Editor
Amy Gammill, M. Ed.

Editorial Project Manager
Elizabeth Morris, Ph.D.

Editor-in-Chief
Sharon Coan, M.S. Ed.

Imaging
Alfred Lau
James Edward Grace

Product Manager
Phil Garcia

Acknowledgments:
Microsoft® Access is a registered trademark of Microsoft Corporation in the United States and/or other countries.
All rights reserved.

Publishers
Rachelle Cracchiolo, M.S. Ed.
Mary Dupuy Smith, M.S. Ed.

Microsoft Access

for

Includes CD ith templates and project samples

Terrified Teachers

Authors

Jan Ray, Ed.D.

Robert Ray, M.S., M.C.P., M.C.T.
(Microsoft Certified Professional and Microsoft Certified Trainer)

Teacher Created Materials, Inc.
6421 Industry Way
Westminster, CA 92683
www.teachercreated.com

©2002 Teacher Created Materials, Inc.
Made in U.S.A.
ISBN-0-7439-3811-9

Teacher Created Materials

Table of Contents

Table of Contents *(cont.)*

Table of Contents *(cont.)*

Table of Contents *(cont.)*

Introduction

Welcome to *Microsoft Access for Terrified Teachers*. You hold in your hands a book that is designed to help you learn how to use this very powerful database program. This book will also help you integrate the use of *Microsoft Access* into your classroom curricula.

What Is a Database?

A database is an organized collection of information or data. We use databases every day in our lives and hardly notice. For example, a telephone book is a database. The address book section of your personal organizer is a database. On your desk, the box you keep with student information jotted down on index cards is a database.

Microsoft Access just looks a little different from more common databases. It is a computerized database—one that can help you store, retrieve, sort, analyze, and print information in just a couple of keystrokes.

What Is *Microsoft Access*?

Microsoft Access is a database management system (DBMS). It is part of the *Microsoft Office Suite* of products that includes *Microsoft Word*, *Microsoft Excel*, *Microsoft PowerPoint*, *Microsoft Outlook*, and more.

Microsoft Access allows you to create and process data. You can add data, change data, and delete data in your database tables.

Using database queries, you can ask *Microsoft Access* questions about your data, such as, "What is the average population of the 50 states?" You will obtain your answer in an instant.

You can create forms in *Microsoft Access*. These forms can be used to enter data, view data, and update data.

You can generate reports based upon the information in your *Microsoft Access* database. These reports are easy to create and are a great way to present your data.

Microsoft Access also allows you to save your database tables and reports as Web pages so the database you and your students create can be shared over the Internet.

Special Note: The version of *Microsoft Access* used to write this book is *Microsoft Access 2000*. If you have a different version, some of the directions may vary slightly, but you will still be able to perform all of the same functions.

What Is in This Book?

Microsoft Access for Terrified Teachers is divided into four sections: **Introduction**, **Getting Started**, **Creating Your Own Database** and **Student Projects**.

Introduction

The **Introduction** to *Microsoft Access for Terrified Teachers* provides you with an overview of this book. You will also learn how the student projects are presented, how to manage your database files, and how to use the CD-ROM found in the back cover of this book.

Getting Started

The **Getting Started** section provides you with a "warm-up" before actually creating your own *Microsoft Access* databases. You will learn how to launch *Microsoft Access*, the terminology associated with the database objects (e.g., tables, forms, and reports), different views on your screen, and how to save and close the database file.

Creating Your Own Database

In **Creating Your Own Database** you will do just that—create a database of your own. You will learn how to design a database table, how to create a database form, how to sort your data within a table, how to create a report, how to query your database, and much, much more.

Student Projects

In **Student Projects** you will find a variety of projects that you can do with your students that incorporate the use of *Microsoft Access* databases. The projects include language arts, mathematics, social studies, science, health and physical education, and the arts activities. All of the projects include template files, so the databases are already designed and built for you. You can use the databases as they are or modify them to meet your specific curricular needs. (Don't worry. You will learn how to modify a database and a form in the **Creating Your Own Database** section.)

All of the database projects include two or three activities, so you can choose to complete one, two, or all three activities with your students. Many of the activities incorporate the use of other software applications, such as *Microsoft Word*, *Microsoft PowerPoint*, and *Microsoft Excel,* as well as the Internet. Step-by-step instructions are provided for all student activities, as well as sample files and template files that you can use right away with your students.

Each database project is presented as follows:

Project Description

In this section you will read a few introductory words and a brief description of the project activities, giving you a quick overview of what you and your students will be doing.

Hardware and Software Needed

In this section you are provided with information about the hardware and software that you will need to complete each activity.

CD-ROM Files

This section provides a table of the files you can use to complete the project. The table includes the title of each file, its description, its associated software application, and the filename. All of the files listed are provided on the CD-ROM found in the back of the book. You will find database files, presentation files, spreadsheet files, resource files, graphic organizers, score sheets, and more.

Materials Needed and File Preparation

In this section you are provided with a list of materials that you will need to complete each activity within the project. You are also given instructions for how to prepare your files for each activity. This may include creating a project folder, opening and saving files from the CD-ROM to the project folder, and more.

Introducing the Project

Here you will find ideas for preparing your students for the project activities. Sample data and step-by-step instructions are provided, so you can demonstrate to your students how to enter information into each project database. Sample projects that draw upon information in each database are also provided for you to share with students.

Producing the Project

Instructions for facilitating the project are provided—from assigning students their research topics and overseeing their data entry to providing "how to" instructions, graphic organizers, and score sheets.

Presenting the Project

In this section, you are provided with ideas for how you and your students can share the completed database projects with others—from posting databases on classroom Web pages to displaying or presenting projects to other classes.

Additional Project Ideas

This section presents other ideas for using your database. After gathering all of that information, you'll see that there are always more fun ways to use your database!

Additional Resources

In this section, you are provided with additional resources that will help you through the project, such as Internet sites where students can safely conduct their research and library books that students can use to gather information in the more traditional manner.

You will find an *Additional Resources* file on the CD-ROM that will make use of the Internet sites easier [filename: **addresrc.doc**]. It contains active hyperlinks to all of the Internet sites listed in the Additional Resources section of each project. You simply have to make sure that your Web browser is active, open the file from the CD-ROM, and click on any Internet site listed that you would like to view. You will automatically go there. Yeah! You won't have to type in those long Internet addresses!

About File Management

Managing all of the files that you create and use on the computer can become overwhelming—even frustrating. The following suggestion may help you with this very important aspect of using the computer:

Before you begin to use this book, create a folder for all of your *Microsoft Access* files. Then as you are instructed to create project folders, you can place all of them in your *Microsoft Access* Projects folder.

Here's how to create your own *Microsoft Access* Projects folder, as well as one project folder within it. Ready?

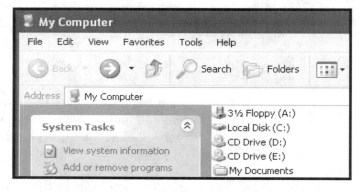

- At your desktop, double-click **My Computer** to open it.

- At the **My Computer** dialog box, double-click the **My Documents** folder to open it.

  Special Note: You may need to first double-click the C: drive icon.

- At the **My Documents** dialog box, click **File** on the **Menu** bar.

- Click **New**.

- Click **Folder**.

- A new folder will appear. You will see the folder name or label **New Folder** highlighted, ready for you to name it.

  Special Note: If the folder is not highlighted, select the **New Folder** icon, then click **File** and **Rename**.

Simply start typing the following: ***Microsoft Access Projects***

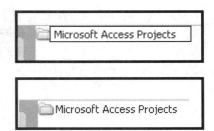

- Then click elsewhere on the screen to view the folder you just created.
- Now double-click your ***Microsoft Access Project folder*** to open it.

- Now you are within the *Microsoft Access* Project folder. Repeat the process for creating a new folder within this folder. It is exactly the same.

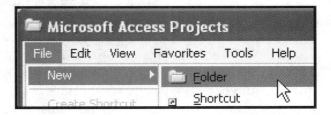

  - Click **File** on the **Menu** bar.
  - Click **New**.
  - Click **Folder**.

- This time, name your folder ***Whales Project***.

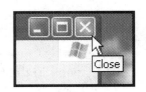

- Now create one more folder called, ***Saluting the States Project***.
- If you have the time, and are so inclined, create several more project folders such as *Presidents Project, Inventions Project*, *Fruit Pie Project*, and *Musical Masters Project* so you feel comfortable creating folders, and are ready for the student projects later in this book.
- When you are finished, click the **Close** button on the **Title** bar to close the *Microsoft Access* Projects folder.

In the **Materials Needed and File Preparation** section of each project, you will find instructions for creating a project folder and saving files to the project folder from the CD-ROM. You can also use the project folders to save any other files related to the project, such as individual student files, clip art files, and more.

About the CD-ROM

Turn to the back of this book and you will find a CD-ROM. It contains the database projects files, resource files, presentation files, spreadsheet files, graphic organizers, scores sheets, and more. The CD-ROM does not contain *Microsoft Access*. The *Microsoft Access* program must be installed on your computer prior to using this book and all the associated files on the CD-ROM.

Special Note: The CD-ROM does not contain *Microsoft Word*, *Microsoft PowerPoint*, *Microsoft Excel*, or Web browser software. Again, these programs must be available on your computer system if you wish to use their associated files from the CD-ROM.

How to Open a File from the CD-ROM

To open a file from the CD-ROM, first carefully remove the CD-ROM from its plastic pouch in the back of this book. Place the CD-ROM in the CD-ROM drive of your computer.

On your computer desktop double-click the **My Computer** icon. When you do, the **My Computer** window opens and displays all the drives on your computer system, such as **C:**, **D:**, and **E:**. Double-click the icon that represents your CD-ROM drive. (You may also see the name of the CD—**tcm_3811**—right next to the CD-ROM drive label. That's helpful!). This action will open the CD-ROM. At the **tcm_3811** window, you will see a list of all the files on the CD-ROM. Just scroll down until you find the file you want and double-click the file to open it. Windows will automatically launch the software application associated with the file if it is available on your computer.

How to Save Files to Your Project Folder

All the files on the CD-ROM are read-only. (That's why it is called a CD-ROM. ROM means Read-Only Memory.) You can open a file from the CD-ROM and use it; however, you cannot save it back to the CD-ROM. So, when you open a file from the CD-ROM, you should immediately save it to the project folder you created on your computer. Here's how you normally save files from a CD-ROM to a project folder:

- Open a file from the CD-ROM, such as the *Saluting the States Research Organizer* [filename: **statesorg.doc**].

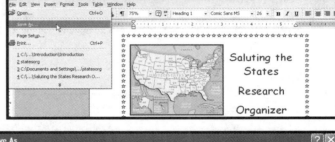

- Before you begin to use the file, click **File** on the **Menu** bar.

- Click **Save As**.

- At the **Save As** dialog box, click the **Save in** list arrow and navigate to your project folder—such as your **Saluting the States Project** folder—and open it.

- Click **Save**.

Now that your file is saved, it is ready for you to use in any way you like. You can print it, modify it, and save it.

Special Note: *Microsoft Access* database files work a little differently than other *Microsoft Office Suite* files, such as those created in *Microsoft Word*, *Microsoft Excel*, and *Microsoft PowerPoint*. With all other *Microsoft Office Suite* files you can use the **Save As** command to save a file from one location to another—like you just did. The Save As command does not work the same in *Microsoft Access*. The Save As command in *Microsoft Access* prompts you to save a Table with a new name. Obviously, that won't get your database file off the CD-ROM and saved into your project folder. So, for the *Microsoft Access* files on the CD-ROM, you have to use a different procedure. Here it is:

- Right-click the *Microsoft Access* database file that you want to save to your project folder.

- When you do, a pop-up, short-cut menu appears.

- Click **Send to**.

- Click **My Documents**.

- Close your CD-ROM window and navigate to your **My Documents** folder.

- You should see the database file listed in your **My Documents** folder.

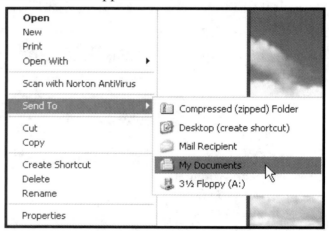

- If you created a *Microsoft Access* **Projects** folder, click and drag the database file into that folder.

  Special Note: If a dialog box pops up, click **Yes**.

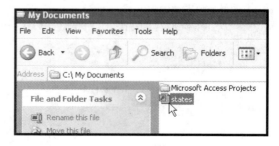

- Double-click the *Microsoft Access* **Projects** folder to open it.
- You should see the database file listed. If you have already created the appropriate project folder, click and drag the database file into that folder.
  Special Note: Again, click **Yes** if a dialog box pops up.

Before you can use the database file, you must remove the Read-only feature. Here's how:

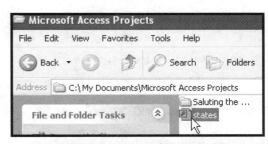

- Right-click the database file and select **Properties**.
- On the **General** tab, deselect the **Read-only** check box by clicking it.
- Click **OK**.
- You're done!

In Conclusion

Well, that's it for your introduction to *Microsoft Access for Terrified Teachers*. I hope you enjoy using the *Microsoft Access* projects and activities with your students as much as I have enjoyed developing them for you.

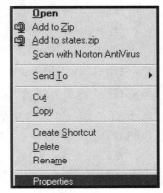

Your feedback on this book is always welcome. You can contact the publisher or me with your comments and suggestions through the Teacher Created Materials Web site at http://www.teachercreated.com. You can e-mail me at drjanray@mindspring.com. I would love to see some of your finished *Microsoft Access* projects and activities!

Getting Started

Before you dive right into the *Microsoft Access* program and the student projects, take a moment to become familiar with the following:

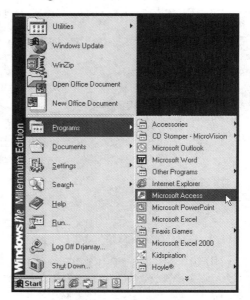

- How to start the *Microsoft Access* program.
- How to identify the components of a database table.
- How to close a database table and file.
- How to exit the *Microsoft Access* program.

Starting *Microsoft Access*

You start *Microsoft Access* the same way you start *Microsoft Word*, *Microsoft Excel*, and other programs on your computer. Here's how:

- Make sure that your computer is turned on and that you see the *Windows* desktop on your screen.
- Click the **Start** button on the taskbar.
- Click **Programs**.
- Click *Microsoft Access*.

Once you start *Microsoft Access*, the *Microsoft Access* program window appears. (This program window will always appear when you start *Microsoft Access*.)

The *Microsoft Access* program window displays a dialog box that provides you with three options. You can:

- open a blank database file and create a database on your own,
- open a blank database file and create a database using the Wizard feature, or
- open an existing database file.

Opening an Existing Database File

First, you will explore an existing database file. Later you will see how to create a database on your own and how to use the Wizard feature.

The database file that you will open is on the CD-ROM that comes with this book. So, carefully remove the CD-ROM from its packaging on the inside back cover, and place it in the CD-ROM drive of your computer.

Since all of the files on the CD-ROM are Read-Only, you will need to first send the database file to your My Documents folder. Remember how to do this? Here's a reminder:

- Click **Open an existing file** in the *Microsoft Access* dialog box.
- Click **OK**.

- In the **Open** dialog box, navigate in the **Look in** list box to the CD-ROM drive that contains the *Microsoft Access for Terrified Teachers* CD. (On my computer system it is the E: drive and TCM_3811 is displayed.)

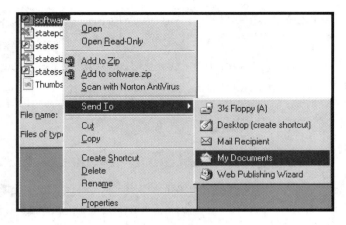

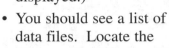

- You should see a list of data files. Locate the *Classroom Software Library* file [filename: **software.mdb**] and right-click it.

- When you do, a pop-up, short-cut menu appears.

- Click **Send to**.

- Click **My Documents**.

- With the **Open** dialog box still displayed, navigate to your **My Documents** folder. You should see the database file listed there.

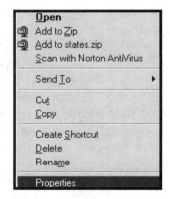

To turn off the Read-only feature on the database file, do the following:

- Right-click the **software.mdb** database file.

- Select **Properties**.

- On the **General** tab, deselect the **Read-only** check box.

- Click **OK.**

To open the *Classroom Software Library* database file:

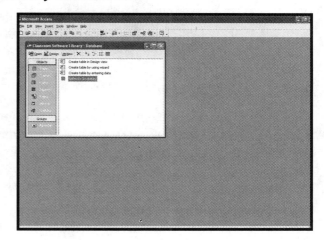

- Click the **software.mdb** file to select it.
- Click **Open.**

The **Classroom Software Library** database window appears on your computer screen. This database window is the main control center for working on the *Classroom Software Library* database.

Reviewing the Opening Screen Components

Before proceeding, you should become familiar with what you see on your screen. Here are the main components:

The *Microsoft Access* Title Bar

At the top of your screen is the *Microsoft Access* title bar. It displays the name of the program you are using—*Microsoft Access.*

The *Microsoft Access* Window Control Buttons

At the far right-hand side of the title bar you will find the Window Control buttons. The Window Control buttons are displayed in two different ways, as shown below. The four Window Control buttons you see are:

- the Minimize button
- the Restore button
- the Maximize button
- the Close button

The Minimize Button

When you click the Minimize button, the *Microsoft Access* program disappears from view. However, it is still running. How can you tell? See the *Microsoft Access* program button displayed on the Taskbar at the bottom of your screen? That's how you can tell. Click the program button on the Taskbar and *Microsoft Access* will reappear on your desktop, ready to use.

 The Minimize button allows you to remove *Microsoft Access* from your screen without closing it, so that you can work with other programs. When you are ready, you can quickly switch back to *Microsoft Access* by clicking the program button on the Taskbar. It's all part of multitasking!

The Restore Button

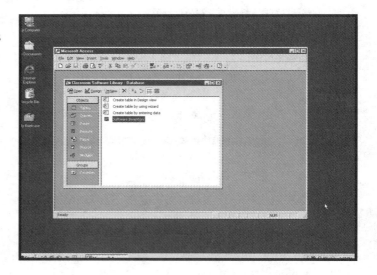

The Restore button indicates that the *Microsoft Access* program window is displayed as large as it can get on your computer screen. When you click the Restore button, the *Microsoft Access* program is reduced, allowing you to see what is behind it. (When teaching, I also refer to this as the "Mediumize" button, because when you click it, your program screen becomes medium-sized.)

Notice that once you click the Restore button, it is no longer displayed. The Restore button has been replaced with a Maximize button.

The Maximize Button

 The Maximize button indicates that your *Microsoft Access* program screen is not displayed at its maximum size. Click the Maximize button and watch the *Microsoft Access* program fill your screen.

Notice that when you click the Maximize button, it is no longer displayed. The Maximize button has been replaced with a Restore button.

The Close Button

 The Close button on the Title Bar allows you to quickly close the *Microsoft Access* program. Click the close button and the *Microsoft Access* program closes and disappears from view.

The Database Window Menu Bar

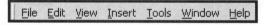 Right below the *Microsoft Access* title bar is the Database Window Menu bar. It includes the following drop-down menus—File, Edit, View, Insert, Tools, Window, and Help. You will learn more about several of the drop-down menus in the Database Window Menu bar as you use them in a subsequent section.

The Database Toolbar

Right below the Database
Window Menu bar is the
Database toolbar. The
Database toolbar displays a
series of buttons or icons that
represent the following
commands or options—New,
Open, Save, Print, Print
Preview, Spell Check, Cut,
Copy, Paste, Format Painter,
Undo, OfficeLinks, Analyze,
Code, Properties,
Relationships, New Object,

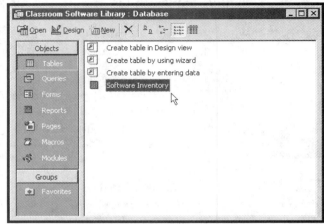

and *Microsoft Access* Help. You will learn more about these buttons or icons in
the Database toolbar in a subsequent section.

The Database Window

Right below the Database toolbar is large gray area. Within the large gray area is
the Database window. This particular Database window contains the *Classroom
Software Library* database you just opened.

The Database Window Title Bar

At the top of the Database window is the Database title bar. Notice that this title
bar looks similar to the *Microsoft Access* title bar. Although they display
different titles, both title bars have the same Window Control buttons.

The Database Window Control Buttons

The Database Window Control buttons work just like the *Microsoft Access* Window Control buttons. The difference is that the Database Window Control buttons control the *Classroom Software Library* file that you just opened. These Window Control buttons minimize, restore, maximize, or close the *Classroom Software Library*  database only. Whereas the *Microsoft Access* Window Control buttons minimize, restore, maximize, or close the entire program.

The Database Window Command and View Buttons

Right below the Database Window title bar are the Command and View buttons.

These buttons change depending upon which object is selected within the Objects bar. (You will learn about the Objects bar in the next section.)

The buttons represent the following commands or view depending on which object is selected: Open, Preview, Run, Design, New, Delete, Large Icons, Small Icons, List, and Details. You will learn more about several of the Database Window Command and View buttons in subsequent sections as you use them.

The Objects Bar

On the left-hand side of the Database window, there is an Objects bar. The Objects bar contains the following *Microsoft Access* objects:

- Tables
  - The Tables object stores data in rows and columns. It is similar to a spreadsheet.

- Queries
  - The Queries object allows you to select and display data. You can even view fields from more than one table.

- Forms
  - The Forms object allows you to create and use a form for inputting data.

- Reports
  - The Reports object allows you to create and print a report of selected field information from your database table.

- Pages
  - The Pages object allows you to publish your database in a simplified form for a Web page.

- Macros
  - The Macros object allows you to automate common database actions.

- Modules
  - The Modules object allows you to automate more complex database operations.

Click each one of these objects and watch the Command buttons change, as well as the objects in the Objects list.

The Groups Bar

Right below the Objects bar is the Groups bar. The Groups bar contains the Favorites folder.

The Objects List

The white box within the Database window lists the objects that are available to you. This list will change depending upon the object you select under the Objects bar.

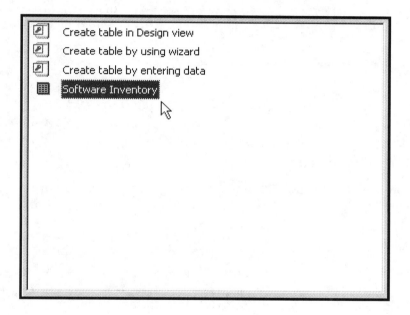

Now that you are familiar with what you see on the *Microsoft Access* screen, complete the opening of the *Classroom Software Library* database.

- Select **Tables** under the **Objects** bar.
- Double-click the **Software Inventory** table within the Objects list to open it.

When you do, the Software Inventory table appears on your screen in Datasheet view. Yes, it does look like a spreadsheet, doesn't it?

As a teacher, you know that every new concept comes with its own list of vocabulary words. So it is with databases. Here are a few key terms to know for any database table you use in *Microsoft Access*:

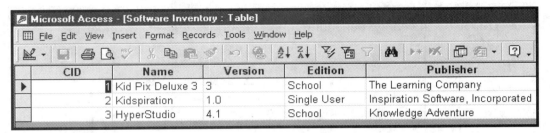

Table

In *Microsoft Access*, database information is entered into tables. As you can see, a table looks similar to a spreadsheet. It has rows, columns, and column headings just like a spreadsheet. The Software Inventory table shown on this page has three rows, 18 columns, and 18 column headings.

Special Note: Not all of the columns are displayed on your screen.

Fields

The columns within a database table are called fields. Fields are attributes of people, places, objects, events, or ideas. There are 18 fields in the *Software Inventory* database shown on this page. Can you name a few of them? If you said CID (Control Identification Number), Name, Version, Edition, and Publisher for the first five fields, you were right!

Field Names

The column headings within the database table are called field names. The field names within the Software Inventory database table shown on this page are CID (Control Identification Number), Name, Version, Edition, and Publisher.

Records

Records are rows of data within the database table. There are three records displayed in the sample *Software Inventory* database table.

Database Views

There are two ways to view a *Microsoft Access* database table—in Datasheet View and in Design View. Right now, you are in Datasheet View.

Datasheet View

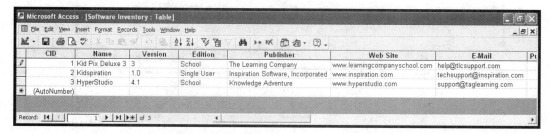

There are a few more screen components in Datasheet View with which you should become familiar before switching to Design View. Here they are:

- There are three record selector symbols that appear next to a record in a database table to indicate its status—the pencil, the triangle, and the asterisk.
  - The **pencil** indicates that the data in this table has not been saved. It also indicates the record within which you are working.
  - **Special Note:** The pencil is probably not displayed on your screen because you have not made any changes to the table.
  - The **triangle** indicates that the data in this table has been saved. It also indicates the record within which you are working.
  - The **asterisk** appears next to a blank record. It is the next record you will use, if you add more records to the database table.

There is a status bar at the bottom of the database table. It displays the number of the record you are working on—the Current Record. It also displays how many records there are in your database.

- Notice that there is a horizontal scroll bar at the bottom of the screen, so that you can view fields that are not displayed.

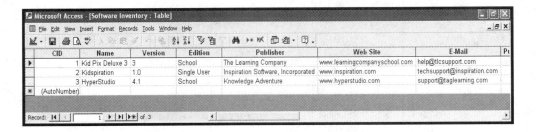

- There are also navigation buttons on the status bar that allow you to move to the beginning of the database, one record to the left, one record to the right, and to the end of the database. There is also a navigation button that allows you to quickly move to the next blank record. This is helpful if you have a very large database and don't want to take the time to scroll down.

- Notice that there are two sets of Window Control buttons in the upper-right-hand corner of the screen. The top set is for the *Microsoft Access* program. The bottom set is for the Software Inventory database table.

Now it's time to take a look at your Software Inventory database table in Design View. To switch to **Design View**, click the **View** button on the *Microsoft Access* toolbar.

Design View

Design View looks quite different from Datasheet View. This is the where the fields within a database table are defined.

There are three columns in the upper pane—Field Name, Data Type, and Description.

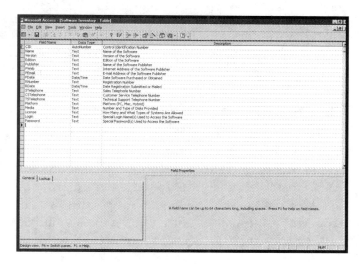

- The Field Name column is where you enter the names of the fields you want in your database. Here are some guidelines for field names:

    - Field names must be unique.

    - Field names can be up to 64 characters.

    - Field names can include letters, numbers, spaces, and some punctuation symbols.

    - Field names cannot contain periods (.), exclamation points (!), or brackets ([]).

- The Data Type column is where you indicate the type of data that will be entered into the field. Depending upon the data type you select, your field may contain letters and numbers, only numbers, numbers with dollar signs, etc. The data types that are used in this *Software Inventory* database include AutoNumber, Text, and Date/Time. Other *Microsoft Access* databases in this book include these three data types plus Memo, Number, Currency, OLE Object, Hyperlink, and Lookup Wizard. Thus, you will become familiar with several data types.

- The Description column is where you enter a detailed description of the field.

In the lower pane (where you see the General and the Lookup tabs), field properties are specified. For example, if my Data Type is Number, I can define the format for the number as standard or scientific. I can also specify how many decimal places to display, such as 0, 1, or 2.

Notice that in this view, there is a triangular row selector (accompanied by a key symbol), so you can clearly see where you are working. There are also the same Window Control buttons that you saw in Datasheet View.

Closing a Database Table and Quitting *Microsoft Access*

To close your database table, click the **Close Window** button. (**Special Note:** Do not click the Close button on the *Microsoft Access* title bar.) You will return to the Classroom Software Library database window. To close the *Classroom Software Library* database file, click the **Close Window** button again. To close *Microsoft Access*, click **File** on the **Menu** bar and select **Exit**, or click the **Close** button on the title bar.

In Conclusion

Now that you are somewhat familiar with launching *Microsoft Access*, opening and closing the database table, and switching between views, it's time for more advanced training. In the next section, ***Creating a Microsoft Access Database***, you will learn how to create a database table in Design View. You will also learn how to create a data entry form and a database report. You will learn how to sort your database and perform queries. Finally, you will learn how to save your database as a Web page, so you can share the data with others. Ready?

Creating Your Own Database

In this section you will create *The Earth* database. Sounds like a broad topic, doesn't it? Well, *The Earth* database is meant to be broad, so that you can experience creating a nice variety of tables, forms, and reports. Once you are finished creating *The Earth* database, you will feel confident enough to venture off and create *Microsoft Access* databases on your own.

So, are you ready to begin? Thought so!

Planning Your Database

Before you jump into creating your own *Microsoft Access* database, it is important to take the time to carefully plan your database. Here are some things that you can do to help you plan your *Microsoft Access* database:

Gathering Data

Start by gathering the data you want to collect and store. Since you will be creating *The Earth* database, begin to gather information about geological features of the earth, such as:

1. continents
2. islands
3. rivers
4. deserts
5. oceans
6. seas
7. lakes
8. mountains

Special Note: Don't feel like you or your students have to gather all this information right now. Just find a few pieces of selected information so that you get the "gist" of this planning step.

Analyzing the Data

Once you have gathered some of the data about the earth, begin analyzing it. Ask yourself:

"How is this information presented?"

"How is this information grouped?"

"How can I (or my students) best group this information?"

Identifying Groups of Information

Once you have identified groups of information, these groups will become your database tables, such as:

1. The Seven Continents
2. The Largest Islands
3. The Longest Rivers
4. The Great Deserts
5. The Four Oceans
6. The Largest Seas
7. The Five Great Lakes
8. The Highest Mountains

Categorizing the Information

Select one of the groups, such as *The Seven Continents*, and determine the information you want gathered and stored in the database table, such as:

1. the name of the continent

2. the area of the continent (in square miles)

3. the rank of the continent in area

4. the rank of the continent in population

These categories of information will become the fields in The Seven Continents table within *The Earth* database.

Select another of the groups, such as *The Highest Mountains*, and determine the information you want gathered and stored in the database table, such as:

1. the name of the mountain

2. the height of the mountain

3. the name of the country in which the mountain is located

4. the name of the continent upon which the mountain is located

These categories of information will become the fields in The Highest Mountains table within *The Earth* database.

Continue in this manner with the other groups to determine the information you want gathered and stored in the database table.

Special Note: Don't feel like you have to do all of this now, as long as you understand how to identify categories of information that will become the fields in your database table.

Looking for Common Elements (Key Fields)

Look for common elements among the tables you have designed. These common elements are called *key fields*. You will use key fields to link tables in your database. Can you find the key field that is common to *The Seven Continents* database table and *The Highest Mountains* database table?

"The name of the continent," you say? That's right!

Designing a Database Table

With the planning phase under your belt, you are ready to begin designing your first database table. Ready to get started? Thought so!

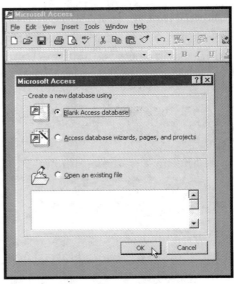

- Launch *Microsoft Access*.
- At the *Microsoft Access* dialog box, select **Blank Access database**.
- Click **OK**.

Naming and Saving Your New Database File

- At the **File New Database** dialog box, click the **Save in** list arrow and navigate to the folder where you would like to save your new database file.

- **Special Note:** It is helpful to have a folder called *The Earth* already created. If you do not, create one now following the instructions in the **About File Management** section of the **Introduction**.

- Click in the **File name** text box and type a name for your new database, such as *The Earth*.

- Click **Create**.

Creating the Database Table in Design View

- At *The Earth* database window, click **Tables** under the **Objects Bar**.
- Click **Create table in Design view** in the **Objects List**.
- Click **Open**.

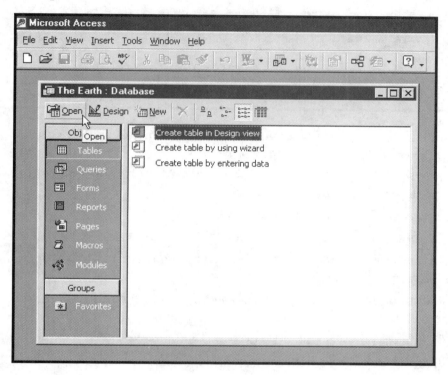

- Once in Design View, maximize your screen by clicking the **Maximize** Window Control button on the **Table** title bar.

Entering Field Names, Data Types, and Descriptions

- Click in the first blank row under **Field Name** and type the following: *Continent*
- Click in or Tab over to the **Data Type** column.
- Click the **Data Type** list arrow and select **Text**, if it is not already selected.
- Click in or Tab over to the **Description** column and type the following: *The name of the continent.*
- Click in or Tab over to the second row in the **Field Name** column and type the following: *Area*

- Click in or Tab over to the **Data Type** column.
- Click the **Data Type** list arrow and select **Number**.

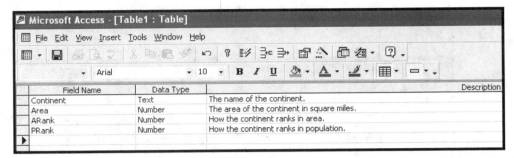

- Click in or Tab over to the **Description** column and type the following: *The area of the continent in square miles.*
- Click in or Tab over to the third row in the **Field Name** column and type the following: *ARank*
- Click in or Tab over to the **Data Type** column.
- Click the **Data Type** list arrow and select **Number**.
- Click in or Tab to the **Description** column and type the following: *How the continent ranks in area.*
- Click in or Tab over to the fourth row in the **Field Name** column and type the following: *PRank*
- Click in or Tab over to the **Data Type** column.
- Click the **Data Type** list arrow and select **Number**.
- Click in or Tab over to the **Description** column and type the following: *How the continent ranks in population.*

Identifying the Primary Key

Before you save the table you created, you must first identify a primary key. A primary key is a field that has unique values. In this table, we will use the **Continent** field as the primary key. No two continents share the same name, so each record within the Continent field will always be unique. Here's how to identify the Continent field as the primary key:

- Click in the row that displays the information about the **Continent** field.

  Special Note: You can tell this row is selected by the black triangle that is pointing to it. The triangle is called a record selector symbol. Other record selector symbols include an asterisk and a pencil.

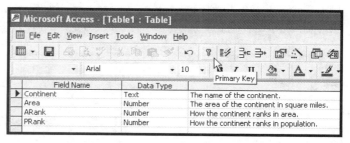

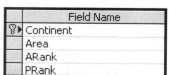

- Click the **Primary Key** button on the **Table** toolbar.

- When you do, notice that the black triangle has been reduced in size and that the primary key symbol now appears next to it.

Naming and Saving the Database Table

Now that the primary key has been identified, you can save your database table.

- Click the **Save** button on the **Table** toolbar.

- At the **Save As** dialog box, type the following in the **Table Name** text box: *The Seven Continents*

- Click **OK**.

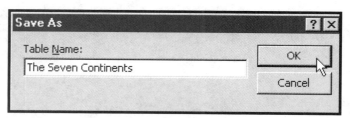

Now that *The Seven Continents* table is named and saved, it is time to go back and "fine-tune" it. You will fine-tune your database table by examining and possibly modifying some of the field properties.

Modifying the Field Properties

At the bottom of your screen, notice the section that is labeled Field Properties. The General tab should be at the forefront. Notice that the Field Size is 50 characters long. This is the default setting for all fields unless you change it.

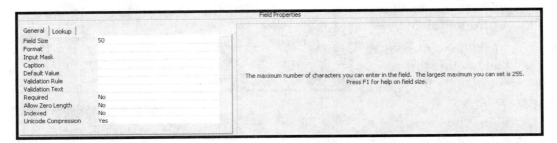

Changing the Field Size

The names of the continents are all far less that 50 characters, so you can save some space in the forms and reports you will be creating shortly by changing 50 to a more reasonable number.

- Click in the **Continent** row under **Field Name** to select it.
- Under **Field Properties**, change the **Field Size** from **50** characters to *20* characters.

Defining the Number Format

Since there are so many ways to present numbers (i.e., with commas or decimals), sometimes defining the Data Type as Number is not enough. You can specify how you want the number to look in your database by formatting it. Here's how:

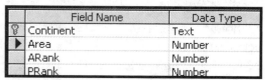

- Click in the **Area** row under **Field Names** to select it.
- Under **Field Properties**, click in the **Format** text box. A list arrow appears.
- Click the **Format** list arrow and select **Standard**.

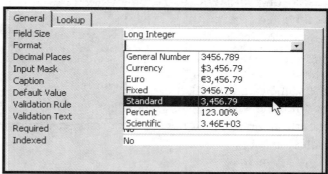

This selection will allow the area values to display commas, which is important when working with large numbers with students. However, notice that the Standard format also displays decimal values. This is not necessary and is inappropriate for large, rounded numbers. So the decimal places should be set to zero.

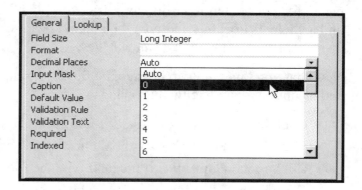

- Click in the **Decimal Places** text box. A list arrow appears.
- Click the **Decimal Places** list arrow and select **0**.

Now the numeric values your students enter in the Area field will be displayed with commas and without decimals.

Creating a Caption

When *The Seven Continents* database table is displayed, the field names will become the column headings in Datasheet View and the labels in Form View. So you want the column headings or labels to clearly represent the information students are to enter into the database table.

Although **Area** is an acceptable column heading or label, it would make it easier for your students if you named it **Area in Square Miles**, so they would clearly understand that they only have to enter the value (e.g., 9,300,000) and not the form of measurement (e.g., square miles) as well.

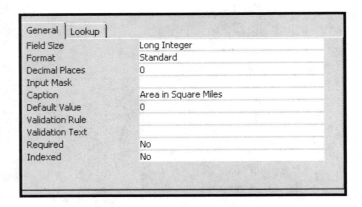

You can tell *Microsoft Access* that you want to use a caption, rather than the field name, for your column heading or label. Simply click in the **Caption** text box under **Field Properties** and type the column heading or label you would like displayed, such as *Area in Square Miles*.

Now that you know how to change the field size, change the number format, and add a caption, complete the following:

- Click in the **ARank** row under **Field Name**.
- Click in the **Field Size** text box, click the list arrow, and select **Integer**.
- Click in the **Caption** text box and type the following: *Rank in Area*
- Click in the **PRank** row under **Field Name**.
- Click in the **Field Size** text box, click the list arrow, and select **Integer**.
- Click in the **Caption** text box and type the following: *Rank in Population*
- Click the **Save** button on the **Table** toolbar to save the changes you made to *The Seven Continents* database.

Adding Information to a Database Table

Now that *The Seven Continents* table is designed, defined, and saved, it's time to add some information or data. In database lingo, this is called *populating* a database.

Changing from Design View to Datasheet View

You have been working in Design View to design and define your database table. In order to begin adding information or data to your database table, you must go to Datasheet View. Here's how:

- Click **View** on the **Menu** bar.
- Click **Datasheet View**.

—or—

- Click the **View** list arrow on the **Tables** toolbar.
- Click **Datasheet View**.

Adjusting the Column (Field) Width in Datasheet View

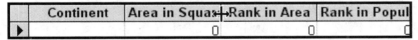

When your database table is displayed in Datasheet View, you may need to immediately resize some of the columns (fields), so that you can see the full column headings or field names. Here's how:

- Move your cursor over the separator line to the right of the column heading that is not fully displayed, such as **Area in Square** shown above.

- When your cursor changes to a resize arrow (as shown to the right), double-click your mouse.

- The column will automatically expand to display the entire heading or field name.
- Now that you know how, resize all of the columns that need resizing.

Entering Data in Datasheet View

Now that you can see the column headings or field names clearly, it's time to start entering data into your database table.

- Click in the first row or record of the **Continent** field.
- Type the following continent name: ***North America***
- Click in or Tab over to the **Area in Square Miles** field.
- Type the following square miles: ***9,300,000***
- Click in or Tab over to the **Rank in Area** field.
- Type the following rank: ***3***
- Click in or Tab over to the **Rank in Population** field.
- Type the following rank: ***4***
- Click in or Tab over to the second row or record of the **Continent** field.
- Type the following continent name: ***South America***
- Click in or Tab over to the **Area in Square Miles** field.
- Type the following: ***6,800,000***
- Click in or Tab over to the **Rank in Area** field.
- Type the following: ***4***
- Click in or Tab over to the **Rank in Population** field.
- Type the following: ***5***
- Click the **Save** button on the **Table** toolbar to save your work.

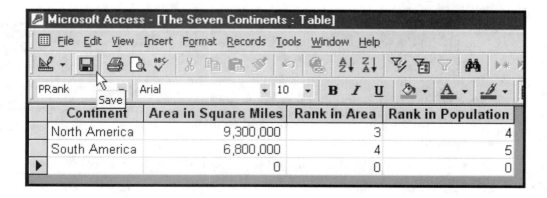

You could continue entering the information for the remaining continents in Datasheet View. However, this is an opportunity for you to explore another way of entering data—in Form View.

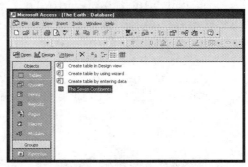

In order to enter data in Form View, you must create a form. Up for the task? Thought so.

Before creating a form, close the database table, so it is out of sight:

- Click **File** on the **Menu** bar.
- Click **Close**.

This action simply closes *The Seven Continents* database table. It does not close *The Earth* database. In fact, once *The Seven Continents* database table is closed, you will return to *The Earth* database command window shown to the right.

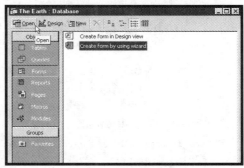

Creating a Database Form

A database form provides a more attractive way to enter, display, and print the information in a table. A form is easy to create and use. Here's how:

- Click **Forms** under the **Objects** bar.
- Click **Create form by using wizard** to select it.
- Click the **Open** command button.

- At the first **Form Wizard** dialog box, select the fields that you want included in your form.

  I recommend including all of them. So, click the double-arrow button that points to the right. It moves all of the fields into the form at once. That's a lot faster than clicking on a field and then clicking on the single-arrow button. That would take ten clicks. With the double-arrow button, you did it in just one click!

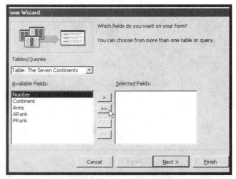

- Once you see that all of the fields have moved from the **Available Fields** box to the **Selected Fields** box, click **Next**.

- At the second Form Wizard dialog box, select the layout you would like for your form. You have four options—Columnar, Tabular, Datasheet, and Justified. Select **Columnar**.

- Then click **Next**.

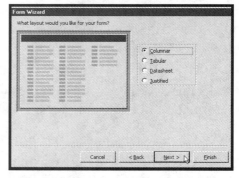

- At the third Form Wizard dialog box, you can select the style for your form. You have several options, such as Blends, Blueprint, Expedition, Industrial, and more. Click through the style options to view them all. Select **International**.

- Then click **Next**.

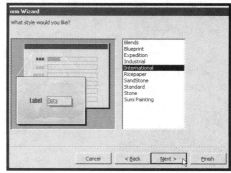

At the fourth Form Wizard dialog box, check to make sure that the title of the form is correct. If it is, just leave it. If it is not, change it.

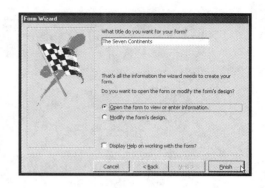

- Then click **Finish**.

Congratulations! Your form is created and ready for some data.

Adding Information to a Database Form

Now that *The Seven Continents* database form is designed and saved, it's time to add more information or data to *The Seven Continents* database. This time you will be adding information in Form View, using the database form you just created, rather than in Datasheet View. Here goes!

- Look at the navigation buttons in the lower left-hand corner of your screen. Notice that you are at Record 1 of 2. Click the **New Record** button to begin Record 3.

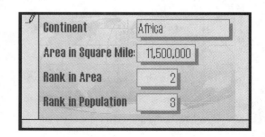

- Enter the following information into Record 3:

- In the **Continent** field, type the following: *Africa*

- In the **Area in Square Miles** field, type the following: *11,500,000*

- In the **Rank in Area** field, type the following: *2*

- In the **Rank in Population** field, type the following: *3*

- Notice that if you press the **<Enter>** key or the **<Tab>** key on your keyboard after entering data into the last field in Record 3, Record 4 automatically pops up. Enter the following information into Record 4:

- In the **Continent** field, type the following: *Europe*
- In the **Area in Square Miles** field, type the following: *3,750,000*
- In the **Rank in Area** field, type the following: *6*

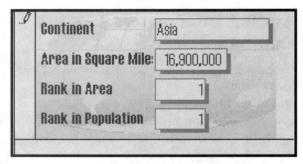

- In the **Rank in Population** field, type the following: *2*

- Enter the following information into Record 5:
  - In the **Continent** field, type the following: *Asia*
  - In the **Area in Square Miles** field, type the following: *16,900,000*

  - In the **Rank in Area** field, type the following: *1*
  - In the **Rank in Population** field, type the following: *1*

- Save your work!

You could continue entering the information for the remaining continents. However, this is an opportunity for you to make some modifications to your database form. Then you can test the changes you made while entering the remaining data.

Modifying the Database Form in Design View

First, let's carefully examine your database form, to identify some things that you can change, such as the following:

1. The database form would look nicer if the background picture was larger. It's hard to tell there is a world behind the labels and data boxes.

2. The database form needs a header, such as ***Continent Information***.

3. The label **Area in Square Miles** is truncated. In database lingo, that means cut off. You can't read the entire label. The label needs to be expanded to display the final *s* in ***Miles***.

4. The form would be easier to read if the font size was larger.

5. Although your students could navigate the database using the navigation buttons in the lower left-hand corner of the screen, there is plenty of room on this form for command buttons, such as Add Record, Find Record, Delete Record, and Close Form. So, let's add them.

Well, these are all easy changes that you can make in Design View. Ready to get started? Thought so.

Changing from Form View to Design View

Right now you are in Form View. To make the changes listed, you have to go to Design View. Here's how:

- Click **View** on the **Menu** bar.
- Click **Design View**.

   —or—

- Click the **View** list arrow on the **Forms** toolbar.
- Click **Design View**.

"Eeek!" you exclaim. "This doesn't look anything like Design View did before."

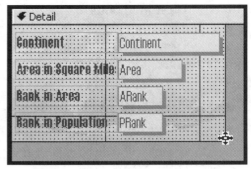

Well, you are right about that. Earlier you were working in Design View for tables. Now you are working in Design View for forms—and it is quite a bit different.

Just take a deep breath—or two, if necessary. It won't be too difficult, I promise.

Expanding the Database Form

To make the form more attractive and to provide room for command buttons, expand the database form. Here's how:

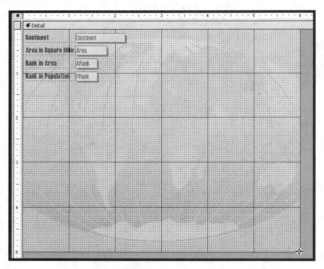

- Maximize the form window by clicking the **Maximize** Window Control button.

- Move your cursor to the lower right-hand corner of the database form. Notice that your cursor changes from a pointer to a resize arrow.

- Using the resize arrow, click and drag the lower right-hand corner of the database form until it is 6 inches wide and 5 inches long. There are horizontal and vertical rulers bordering the database form to help you obtain these measures.

- Save your work!

Now see, that wasn't so hard.

Adding and Formatting a Form Header

Adding a header to a database form is like adding a title to a report. Here's how:

- Right-click anywhere on your database form. When you do, a pop-up menu appears.

- Click on **Form Header/Footer**. When you do, the space for a form header appears at the top of your database form.

   Special Note: If it is not visible, scroll up to the top of the form.

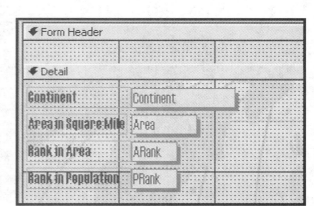

- Click the **Toolbox** button on the **Form View** toolbar. When you do, a Toolbox window appears with a variety of command buttons.

- Click the **Label** button.

- Move your cursor to the form header space. Notice that your cursor has changed to a cross hair, accompanied by the letter A.

- Position the **A** where you would like the first letter of your header to appear.

- Click in the form header space.

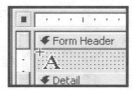

- Type the following: ***Continent Information***

  Special Note: Don't be alarmed if you can barely read what you are typing. The brown background behind your typing is normal. It will disappear shortly.

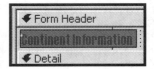

- Click elsewhere on the screen to view the form header you just entered.

The form header needs some additional formatting to stand out as a header. So, let's make a few changes.

Changing the Font Size of a Form Header

One way to make the form header stand out is to change the font size, making it larger. Here's how:

- Click the **Continent Information** form header to select it.
- Click the **Font Size** list arrow on the **Formatting** toolbar.
- Select **24** point. When you do, notice that the form header is only partially displayed. It is now larger than the space provided.

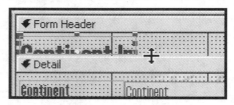

Resizing the Form Header Space

You will need to increase the space so the form header displays nicely. Here's how:

- Move your cursor to the top of the **Detail** bar. When you do, notice that your cursor changes from a pointer to a vertical resize arrow.
- Using the resize arrow, click and drag the top of the **Detail** bar down a bit.

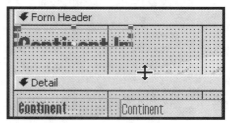

Centering the Form Header

Now that you have room for the form header, resize it in such a way that it can be centered across the top of the database form. Here's how:

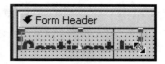

- Move your cursor over the select button in the lower right-hand corner of the form header text. When you do, your pointer changes to a diagonal resize arrow.

- Using the resize arrow, click and drag the select button all the

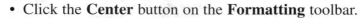
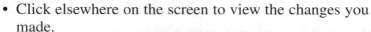

way to the lower right-hand corner of the form header space.

- Click the **Center** button on the **Formatting** toolbar.

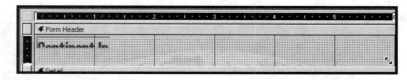

- Click elsewhere on the screen to view the changes you made.

- Click the **Close** button on the **Toolbox** window.

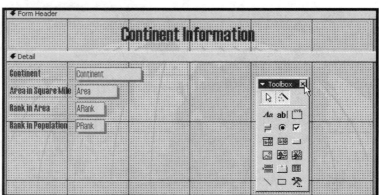

Resizing a Form Label

Okay, it's time to expand the **Area in Square Miles** label so that all the letters are displayed. Ready?

Selecting Multiple Controls

Before resizing the form label, you need to make more room for it by moving the **Area** control to the right. So that your form remains uniform, all the controls need to be moved to the right.

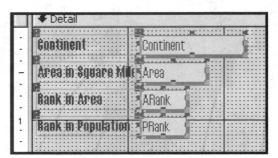

- Select all the controls. Here's how to select multiple controls:
  - Click the **Continent** control to select it. When you do, notice the select handles that appear.
  - Hold down the **<Shift>** key on your keyboard and click the **Area** control, the **ARank** control, and the **PRank** control.

Grouping Controls

Now that all the controls are selected, group them. Grouping the controls allows you to move them all at once. This eliminates the need for aligning individually moved controls—which can take a lot of time.

- Click **Format** on the **Menu** bar.
- Click **Group**. When you do, notice that all the individual select handles disappeared. One set of select handles surrounding the grouped controls appears.

Moving Controls

Now that all the controls are grouped, move them.

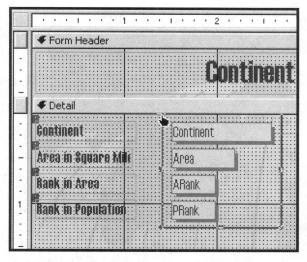

- Move your pointer over the select handle in the upper left-hand corner. Notice that your pointer changes to a hand.

- When you see the hand, click and drag the controls to the right—to about the 1.5-inch mark on the ruler.

Selecting and Resizing a Form Label

Now there is room to expand the Area in Square Miles label.

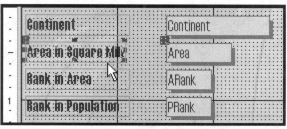

- Click the **Area in Square Miles** label to select it. When you do, notice the select handles that appear.

- Move your pointer to the middle select button on the right-hand side of the **Area in Square Miles** label. Notice that your pointer changes to a horizontal resize arrow.

- When you see the horizontal resize arrow, click and resize the **Area in Square Miles** label to the right— just enough to see all the letters.

Taking a Peek at the Changes

Would you like to view the changes you have made so far? Thought so.

- Click the **Form View** button on the **Form Design** toolbar to go to Form View.

- When you are finished viewing, click the **Design View** button on the **Form View** toolbar to continue modifying your form.

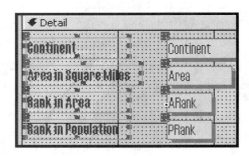

Enlarging the Font Size of Form Labels and Controls

Your form will be easier to read if the form labels and controls are larger. Right now, the default font size for the form labels is 12 points and the default font size for the form controls is 11 points. Let's make the form labels 16 points and the controls 14 points. Ready?

Selecting Multiple Form Labels

Select all the form labels at once, so that you can change their font size with one command. Here's how:

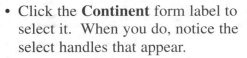

- Click the **Continent** form label to select it. When you do, notice the select handles that appear.

- Hold down the **<Shift>** key on your keyboard and click the **Area in Square Miles** label, the **Rank in Area** label, and the **Rank in Population** label.

Enlarging the Font Size of Selected Form Labels

Now that all the form labels are selected, resize them.

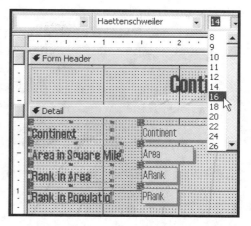

- Click the **Font Size** list arrow on the **Formatting** toolbar.
  Special Note: If you don't see the **Formatting** toolbar on your screen, here's how to make it appear:
  - Click **View** on the **Menu** bar.
  - Click **Toolbars**.
  - Click **Formatting (Form/Report)**.

    The Formatting toolbar now appears above the horizontal ruler on your Form View screen.

- Click **16** points.

Resizing Multiple Form Labels

Now that your form labels are 16 points, two of them are truncated. So, while they are all still selected, resize them—both at once.

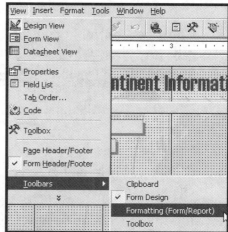

- Just as you did before, move your pointer to the middle select button on the right-hand side of the **Area in Square Miles** label. Notice that your pointer changes to a horizontal resize arrow.

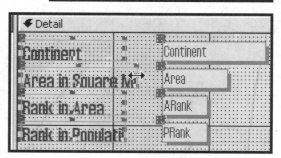

- When you see the horizontal resize arrow, click and resize the **Area in Square Miles** label to the right—just enough to see all the letters.

- Notice that since all the form labels were selected, they were all resized, including the other truncated form label—Rank in Population. So, you are done!

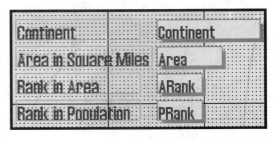

Enlarging the Font Size of Selected Controls

Now that the form labels are resized, it's time to resize the controls.

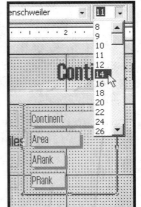

- Click the **Continent** control to select it. Notice that since you grouped the controls earlier, all are automatically selected.

- Click the **Font Size** list arrow on the **Formatting** toolbar.

- Click **14** points.

- Click elsewhere on the screen to view the font changes you made.

Resizing the Form Labels and Controls Vertically

Notice that some of the letters are not fully displayed vertically, such as the tail of the *q* in *Square* and the tail of the *p* in *Population*. It's quick and easy to resize the form labels and controls vertically. Here's how:

- Click **Edit** on the **Menu** bar.
- Click **Select All**.

- Notice that everything on your screen is selected, including the header Continent Information. Since you don't want to change the size of this header in any way, deselect it. Here's how:

  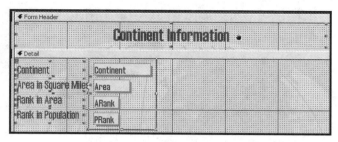

  - Hold down the **<Shift>** key on your keyboard.
  - Click on **Continent Information** to deselect it.

- Now that just the form labels and controls are selected, move your pointer to the middle select button at the bottom of the **Rank in Population** label. Notice that your pointer changes to a vertical resize arrow.

  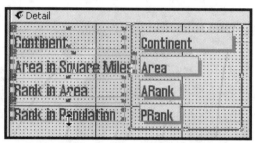

- When you see the vertical resize arrow, click and resize the **Rank in Population** label down—just enough to see full tail of the letter **p**.

  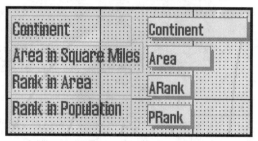

- Notice that since all the form labels and controls were selected, they were all resized, including **Area in Square Miles**. So, you are done!

  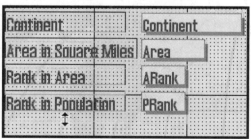

- Click elsewhere on the screen to view the changes you made. Much nicer!

Adding Command Buttons Using the Command Button Wizard

Let's add four command buttons to your form—Add Record, Find Record, Delete Record, and Close Form. Adding command buttons is not a hard task to perform, I promise! It's easy when you use the Command Button Wizard.

Displaying the Toolbox Window

You can access the Command Button Wizard through the Toolbox window. So, let's display it:

- Click the **Toolbox** button on the **Form Design** toolbar. The Toolbox window appears on your screen.

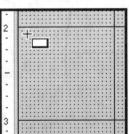

- If necessary, move the **Toolbox** window out of your work area:
    - Click the **Toolbox** window title bar and move it to the top of your screen, out of the way.

Creating the Add Record Command Button

Ready to add your first command button? You will start with the Add Record command button.

- Click the **Command Button** within the **Toolbox** window.
- Move your pointer—which is now displayed as a cross hair and a small command button—to about the 2-inch vertical rule line and click. When you do, a command button appears on your screen.

My command button displays *Command12*. Your command button may display *Command1* or some other number. That's okay. You will be changing the text on the command button in just a few seconds.

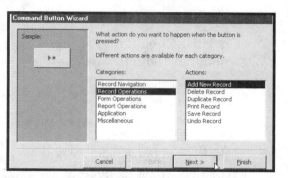

- The first **Command Button Wizard** dialog box is also displayed. Under **Categories**, click **Record Operations**.
- Under **Actions**, click **Add New Record**.
- Click **Next**.
- At the second Command Button Wizard dialog box, click **Text**.
- Click **Next**.

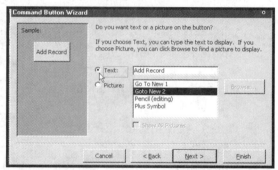

- At the third Command Button Wizard dialog box, click in the textbox and remove the command button name that is displayed.
- Type: *Add Record*
- Click **Finish**.

Congratulations! The Add Record command button now appears on your screen.

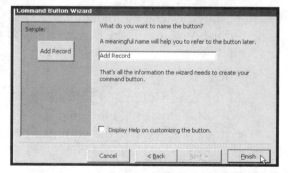

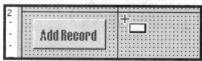

Adding the Find Record Command Button

Ready for your second command button? This one will be even easier:

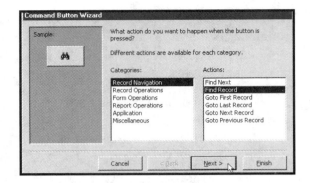

- Click the **Command Button** within the **Toolbox** window.
- Move your pointer—which is now displayed as a cross hair and a small command button—to the right of the Add Record button and click. When you do, a second command button appears on your screen.
- At the first Command Button Wizard dialog box, click **Record Navigation** under **Categories**.
- Under **Actions**, click **Find Record**.
- Click **Next**.
- At the second Command Button Wizard dialog box, click **Text**.
- Click **Next**.
- At the third Command Button Wizard dialog box, click in the textbox and remove the command button name that is displayed.

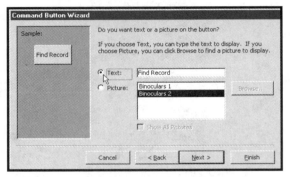

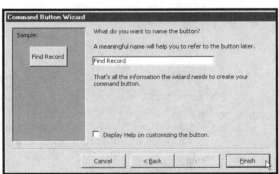

- Type: *Find Record*
- Click **Finish**.

Click elsewhere on the screen to view the second command button you created. Don't worry if the two command buttons aren't lined up vertically or horizontally. We'll fix that later.

Yeah! Two down. Two to go.

Adding the Delete Record Command Button

Ready for your third command button? Thought so.

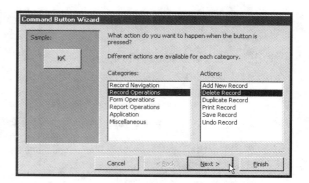

- Click the **Command Button** within the **Toolbox** window.
- Move your pointer—which is now displayed as a cross hair and a small command button—to the right of the Find Record button and click. When you do, a third command button appears on your screen.
- At the first Command Button Wizard dialog box, click **Record Operations** under **Categories**.
- Under **Actions**, click **Delete Record**.
- Click **Next**.

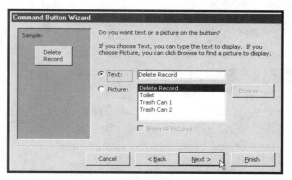

- At the second Command Button Wizard dialog box, click **Text**.
- Click **Next**.
- At the third Command Button Wizard dialog box, click in the textbox and remove the command button name that is displayed.

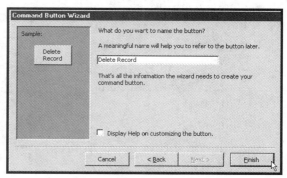

- Type: *Delete Record*
- Click **Finish**.
- Click elsewhere on the screen to view the changes you made.

Adding the Close Form Control Button

Now let's add the fourth and final command button:

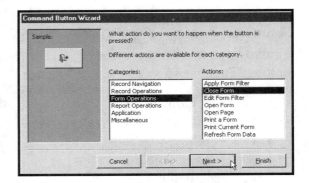

- Click the **Command Button** within the **Toolbox** window.

- Move your pointer—which is now displayed as a cross hair and a small command button—to the right of the Delete Record button and click. When you do, a fourth command button appears on your screen.

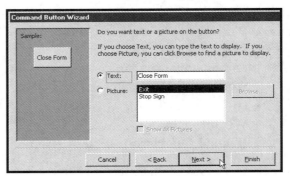

- At the first Command Button Wizard dialog box, click **Form Operations** under **Categories**.

- Under **Actions**, click **Close Form**.

- Click **Next**.

- At the second Command Button Wizard dialog box, click **Text**.

- Click **Next**.

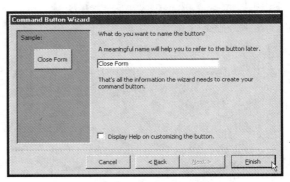

- At the third Command Button Wizard dialog box, click in the textbox and remove the command button name that is displayed.

- Type: *Close Form*

- Click **Finish**.

That's it! Click elsewhere on the screen to view the four command buttons you created.

Aligning and Spacing the Command Buttons

Your command buttons probably need a little straightening out. Don't worry.
You don't have to nudge them up, down, to the right, and to the left, until they line up perfectly. You can let the *Microsoft Access* program do that for you.

Selecting Multiple Command Buttons

- First you have to select all the command buttons.
- Hold down the **<Shift>** key on your keyboard.
- Click the **Add Record** command button.
- Click the **Find Record** command button.
- Click the **Delete Record** command button.
- Click the **Close Form** command button.
- Release the **<Shift>** key.

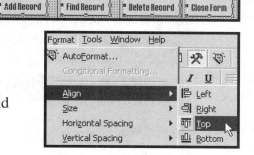

Aligning the Command Buttons

To align the command buttons so that they line up evenly at the top:

- Click **Format** on the **Menu** bar.
- Click **Align**.
- Click **Top**.

Spacing the Command Buttons

To space the command buttons evenly:

- Click **Format** on the **Menu** bar.
- Click **Horizontal Spacing**.
- Click **Make Equal**.

When you click elsewhere on the screen, your command buttons should look nicely aligned and evenly spaced on your screen. Do they?

Now that you are done creating command buttons, you can close the Toolbox window. Click the **Close** button and it will disappear from view.

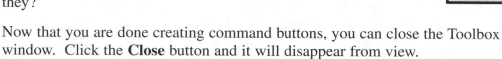

Adding Information to a Modified Database Form

Now that you have modified your database form, it's time to add more data. So switch from Design View to Form View, and let's get started.

When you return to Form View, notice that you are on Record 1 of 5. You have already entered 5 of the 7 continents. Just two more to go.

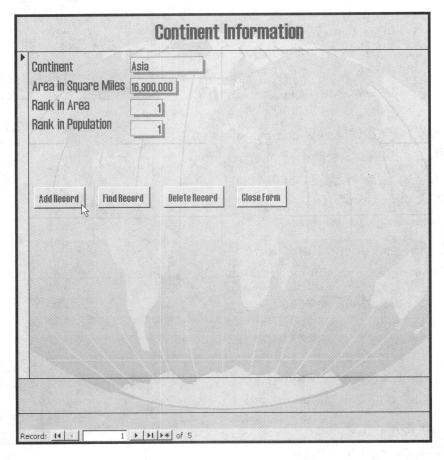

- Click the **Add Record** button, and *Microsoft Access* will automatically take you to Record 6—a new record.
- Enter the following information into Record 6:
  - In the **Continent** field, type the following: *Australia*
  - In the **Area in Square Miles** field, type the following: *2,968,000*

- In the **Rank in Area** field, type the following: *7*
- In the **Rank in Population** field, type the following: *6*
- Click **Add Record**. *Microsoft Access* will automatically take you to Record 7—a new record.

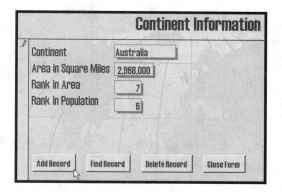

- Enter the following information into Record 7:
  - In the **Continent** field, type the following: *Antarctica*
  - In the **Area in Square Miles** field, type the following: *5,300,000*
  - In the **Rank in Area** field, type the following: *5*
  - In the **Rank in Population** field, type the following: *7*

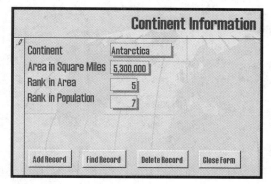

Congratulations! You have just completed your first *Microsoft Access* database table.

No sitting on your laurels yet! Now that your first database table is complete, you will create a second database table that shares information with the first, making your database truly relational.

Now click the **Close** Window Control button. When you do, you will return to
The Earth database window.

Creating a Second Database Table

Watch how much easier your second database table will be to create. Ready to
get started? Thought so!

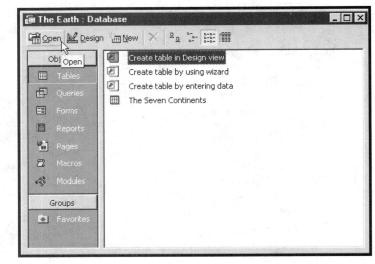

- At **The Earth**
  database window,
  click **Tables** under
  Objects.
- Click **Create
  table in Design
  view** under the
  Objects list.
- Click **Open**.
- Once in Design
  View, if it is not
  maximized
  already, maximize
  your screen by
  clicking the **Maximize** Window Control button on the **Table** title bar.

Entering Field Names, Data Types, and Descriptions

- Click in the first blank row under **Field Name** and type the following:
  Mountain
- Click in or Tab over to the **Data Type** column.
- Click the **Data Type** list arrow and select **Text**.
- Click in or Tab over to the **Description** column and type the following:
  The name of the mountain.
- Click in or Tab over to the second row in the **Field Name** column and type
  the following: *Height*

- Click in or Tab over to the **Data Type** column.
- Click the **Data Type** list arrow and select **Number**.

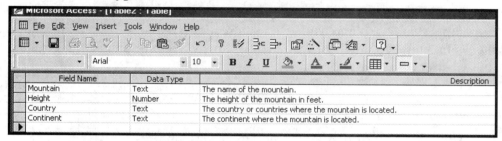

Field Name	Data Type	Description
Mountain	Text	The name of the mountain.
Height	Number	The height of the mountain in feet.
Country	Text	The country or countries where the mountain is located.
Continent	Text	The continent where the mountain is located.

- Click in or Tab over to the **Description** column and type the following: *The height of the mountain in feet.*
- Click in or Tab over to the third row in the Field Name column and type the following: *Country*
- Click in or Tab over to the **Data Type** column.
- Click the **Data Type** list arrow and select **Text**.
- Click in or Tab to the **Description** column and type the following: *The country or countries where the mountain is located.*
- Click in or Tab over to the fourth row in the **Field Name** column and type the following: *Continent*

  Special Note: Yes, you used this field name in *The Seven Continents* database table. So, this is where you will create a relationship between the two tables—in a little while.

- Click in or Tab over to the **Data Type** column.
- Click the **Data Type** list arrow and select **Text**.
- Click in or Tab over to the **Description** column and type the following: *The continent where the mountain is located.*

Identifying the Primary Key

Before you save the second table you created, you must first identify a primary key. In this table, we will use the **Mountain** field as the primary key. No two mountains share the same name, so each record within the Mountain field will always be unique. Here's how to identify the Mountain field as the primary key—just in case you forgot:

- Click in the row that displays the information about the **Mountain** field.
- Click the **Primary Key** button on the **Table** toolbar.
- When you do, notice that the black triangle has been reduced in size and that the primary key symbol now appears next to it.

Naming and Saving the Second Database Table

Now that the primary key has been identified, you can save your second database table.

- Click the **Save** button on the **Table** toolbar.
- At the **Save As** dialog box, click in the **Table Name** text box and type the following: ***The Highest Mountains***
- Click **OK**.

Now that *The Highest Mountains* table is named and saved, it is time to go back and "fine-tune" your second database table. Let's examine and modify some of the field properties.

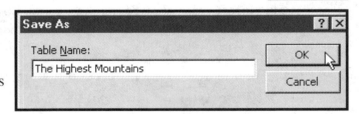

Modifying the Field Properties

Make the following changes to the field properties in your second database table. Review the instructions from your first database table if you don't remember how to perform a task. The new task—creating a lookup column that links the two database tables—will be thoroughly explained.

- For the **Mountain** field, change the **Field Size** to *25*.
- For the **Height** field, change the **Format** to **Standard**.
- Change the **Decimal Places** to *0*.
- Add the following **Caption**: *Height in Feet*
- For the **Country** field, change the **Field Size** to *25*.
- For the **Continent** field, change the **Field Size** to *25*.

Good Work!

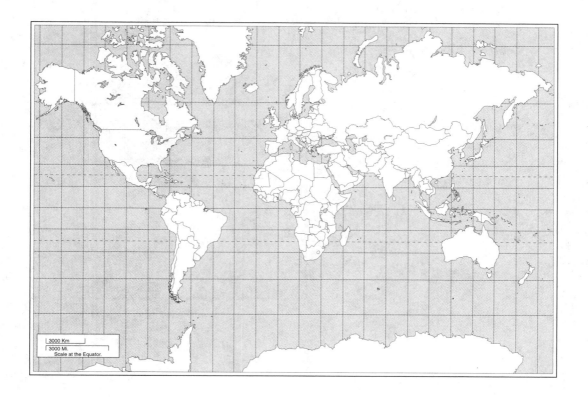

Creating a Lookup Column

Ready for something new? Using the Lookup Wizard, you can create a lookup column for the Continent field. Here's how:

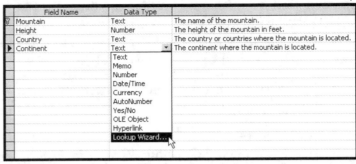

- In the **Continent** field, click the **Data Type** list arrow and select **Lookup Wizard**.

- At the first Lookup Wizard dialog box, click **I want the lookup column to look up the values in a table or query**.

- Then click **Next**.

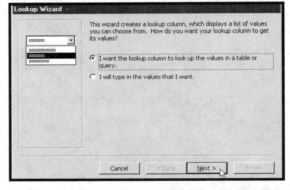

- In the second Lookup Wizard dialog box, **The Seven Continents** database table should already be selected for you, since it is the only other table available in *The Earth* database. So, simply click **Next**.

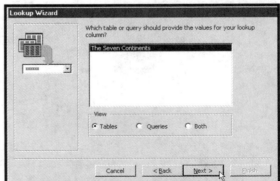

At the third Lookup Wizard
dialog box, click **Continent**
under **Available Fields**.

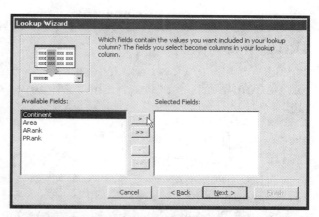

- Click the right arrow. This
  will move the **Continent**
  field into the **Selected
  Fields** list.
- Click **Next**.
- At the fourth Lookup
  Wizard dialog box, you
  have the opportunity to
  widen the lookup column.
  Since all the continents are
  displayed with ample space,
  click **Next**.

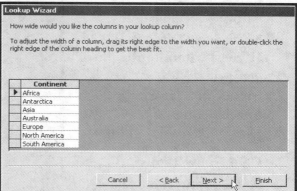

- At the fifth Lookup Wizard
  dialog box, you have the
  opportunity to provide a
  label for the lookup column.
  Type *Continent* in the
  lookup column text box, if it
  is not already displayed.
- Click **Finish**.
- You will be prompted to
  save your database table, so
  that the relationship can be
  created. Click **Yes**.

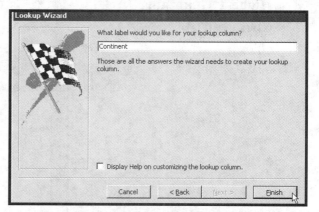

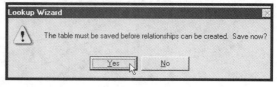

Viewing the Relationship Between Database Tables

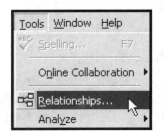

Would you like to view the relationship between **The Seven Continents** and **The Highest Mountains** database tables? Here goes:

- Click **Tools** on the **Menu** bar.
- Click **Relationships**.
- The Relationships window opens and displays the fields of the **The Seven Continents** table.

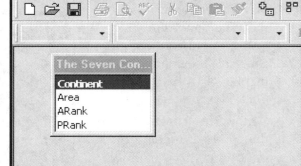

- To display the fields of **The Highest Mountains** table as well, click **View** on the **Menu** bar.

  Special Note: It may already be displayed for you.

- Click **Show Table**.
- At the **Show Table** dialog box window, click **The Highest Mountains**.
- Click **Add**.
- Click **Close**.

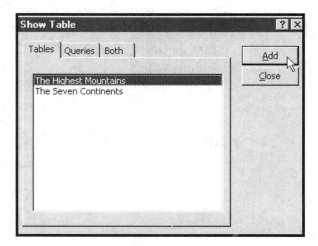

Notice that the two database tables are now displayed side-by-side in the **Relationships** window. Also, notice that there is a line connecting the **Continent** field in **The Seven Continents** table to the **Continent** field in **The Highest Mountains** table. This line shows how the two database tables are related—through the Continent field.

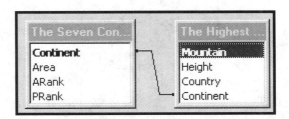

- To close the Relationships window, click the **Close Window** button at the end of the **Menu** bar. (Careful! Don't click the **Close** button on the **Title** bar by mistake.)
- You may be prompted to save changes to the Relationships layout. If so, click **Yes**.

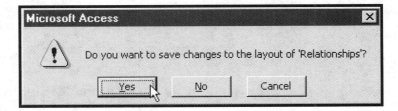

Adding Information to a Second Database Table

Now that *The Highest Mountains* database table is designed, defined, and saved, it's time to add some information or data. Ready to populate your database table?

Entering Data in Datasheet View

- First, switch to **Datasheet View**.
- Click in the first row or record of the **Mountain** field.
- Type the following mountain name: *Everest*
- Click in or Tab over to the **Height in Feet** field.
- Type the following height: *29,028*
- Click in or Tab over to the **Country** field.
- Type the following countries: *Nepal and Tibet*
- Click in or Tab over to the **Continent** field.
- Click the list arrow and select **Asia**.

Special Note: This is the lookup column information you created when designing *The Highest Mountains* database. Your students can now simply select the continent rather than typing its name.

- Click in or Tab over to the second row or record of the **Mountain** field.
- Type the following mountain name: *Aconcagua*
- Click in or Tab over to the **Height in Feet** field.
- Type the following height: *22,834*
- Click in or Tab over to the **Country** field.
- Type the following country: *Argentina*

- Click in or Tab over to the **Continent** field.
- Click the list arrow and select **South America**.
- Click in or Tab over to the third row or record of the **Mountain** field.
- Type the following mountain name: *McKinley*
- Click in or Tab over to the **Height in Feet** field.
- Type the following height: *20,320*
- Click in or Tab over to the **Country** field.
- Type the following country: *United States*
- Click in or Tab over to the **Continent** field.
- Click the list arrow and select **North America**.
- Click in or Tab over to the fourth row or record of the **Mountain** field.
- Type the following mountain name: *Kilimanjaro*
- Click in or Tab over to the **Height in Feet** field.
- Type the following height: *19,340*
- Click in or Tab over to the **Country** field.
- Type the following: *Tanzania*
- Click in or Tab over to the **Continent** field.
- Click the list arrow and select **Africa**.

- Click in or Tab over to the fifth row or record in the **Mountain** field.
- Type the following mountain name: *Elbrus*
- Click in or Tab over to the **Height in Feet** field.
- Type the following height: *18,481*
- Click in or Tab over to the **Country** field.
- Type the following: *Russia and Georgia*
- Click in or Tab over to the **Continent** field.
- Click the list arrow and select **Europe**.
- Click in or Tab over to the sixth row or record in the **Mountain** field.
- Type the following mountain name: *Vinson-Massif*
- Click in or Tab over to the **Height in Feet** field.
- Type the following height: *16,869*
- Click in or Tab over to the **Country** field.
- Since there is no official country, leave this field blank.
- Click in or Tab over to the **Continent** field.
- Click the list arrow and select **Antarctica**.
- Click in or Tab over to the seventh row or record in the **Mountain** field.
- Type the following mountain name: *Kosciusko*

Mountain	Height in Feet	Country	Continent
Everest	29,028	Nepal and Tibet	Asia
Aconcagua	22,834	Argentina	South Americ
McKinley	20,320	United States	North Americ
Kilimanjaro	19,340	Tanzania	Africa
Elbrus	18,481	Russia and Geo	Europe
Vinson-Massif	16,860		Antarctica
Kosciusko	7,316	Australia	Australia
	0		

- Click in or Tab over to the **Height in Feet** field.
- Type the following height: *7,316*
- Click in or Tab over to the **Country** field.
- Type the following: *Australia*
- Click in or Tab over to the **Continent** field.
- Click the list arrow and select **Australia**.
- Save your work!
- Certainly, there are other high mountains that you could enter, such as Godwin-Austen, Kanchejunga, Lhotse, and Maklu. However, that's enough to see how your *The Highest Mountains* database table is working.

Adjusting the Column (Field) Width in Datasheet View

Notice that two of the columns are not wide enough to display all the data you entered—the Country field and the Continent field. Adjust the column (field) width so that their contents are fully displayed.

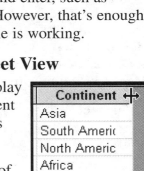

- Move your cursor over the separator line to the right of the **Continent** column heading.
- When your cursor changes to a resize arrow (as shown to the right), double-click your mouse.
- The column will automatically expand to display the entire heading or field.
- Do the same at the **Country** column heading.

Now that you have populated *The Highest Mountains* database table, save it, print it, and close it. You should return to **The Earth** database window.

Sorting within a Database Table

Sorting within a database table allows you to look at the information you entered in different ways. Sorting also helps you prepare to display your information in a database report. So, ready to learn about sorting? Thought so.

In *Microsoft Access* you can sort a single field or multiple fields in your database table. You can sort in either ascending order or descending order.

Sorting in ascending order means your data will be displayed from A to Z if your data is text and can be sorted alphabetically. Your data will be displayed from 1 to 100 (or the largest number in the field) if it can be sorted numerically.

Sorting in descending order means your data will be displayed from Z to A if your data is text and can be sorted alphabetically. Your data will be displayed from 100 (or the largest number in the field) to 1 if it can be sorted numerically.

- Double-click **The Seven Continents** database table to open it.

Continent	Area in Square Miles	Rank in Area	Rank in Population
Asia	16,900,000	1	1
Africa	11,500,000	2	3
North America	9,300,000	3	4
South America	6,800,000	4	5
Antarctica	5,300,000	5	7
Europe	3,750,000	6	2
Australia	2,968,000	7	6

- Examine **The Seven Continents** database table to see if you can identify two columns (fields) that are already sorted. Did you find them? They are:

- **Area in Square Miles**
- **Rank in Area**

  Special Note: These may not be the columns that are sorted in your table. If not, try to identify the column(s) that are sorted.

• Examine these two fields even more closely to see if you can identify the order in which they were sorted—ascending or descending.

The Area in Square Miles field is sorted in descending order. The Rank in Area field is sorted in ascending order. Both fields are sorted numerically.

• To practice sorting *The Seven Continents* database table, move your cursor over the **Continent** column heading. When you do, notice that your cursor changes to a down select arrow.

Special Note: If the Continent column is already sorted in your table, choose another column to sort, such as the Area in Square Miles column.

• When you see the down select arrow, click your mouse to select the entire column.

• Click **Records** on the **Menu** bar.

• Click **Sort**.

• Click **A-Z Sort Ascending**.

• Notice that the Continent column is now displayed in alphabetical order. Also notice that the other columns that were once in order by Area in Square Miles and Rank in Area are no longer in order. That's okay. These columns had to change to accommodate your command to display the Continent column in alphabetical order.

Practice sorting by other fields until you feel comfortable using this *Microsoft Access* feature. When you are finished, close this table. You should return to **The Earth** database window.

Now that you know how to sort your database table, you will use this skill when preparing a report. Ready?

Creating a Database Report

Certainly, you can print a single record or all records from your database at any time. However, the information you print will look like a single row or multiple rows of a spreadsheet. Not too attractive!

Also, when you print a single record or all records of your database, you have no control over the fields and their order. There may be fields you want to exclude from your printout. You may want selected fields to display in a particular order. Regular printing won't allow you to have control of either!

So, *Microsoft Access* has a report feature that allows you to design and generate reports that are more attractive. This feature also allows you to have control over the information reported. Much nicer, eh?

Prior to creating a report, however, it is a good idea to look at the information in your database table. See if the information is sorted just the way you want it to appear in a report. So, open **The Highest Mountains** database table, and let's get started!

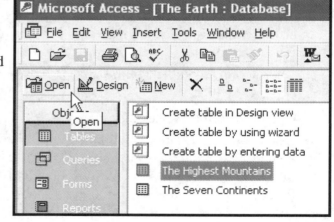

- At **The Earth** database window, click **The Highest Mountains** to select it.
- Click **Open**.

Before proceeding, take a moment to think about the report you want to generate. What fields should be included? What fields should be excluded? How should the data be sorted for display?

For this report, we will only use three fields—the Mountain field, the Country field, and the Height in Feet field. So, the Continent field will be excluded.

As far as how the data should be displayed, the report will have the mountains listed by height, with the tallest mountain listed first and the shortest mountain listed last. So, to prepare for this report, sort the **Height in Feet** field in descending order. Here's how:

- Select the **Height in Feet** field.

- Click **Records** on the **Menu** bar.

- Click **Sort**.

- Click **Z-A Sort Descending**. (Remember, this sorts from the largest to the smallest.)

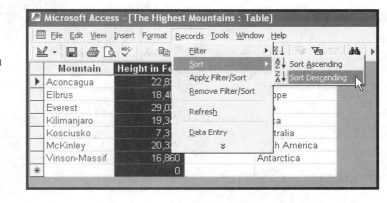

Notice that the mountains are now listed from the highest to the shortest. Now you are ready to generate a report.

- Close **The Highest Mountains** database table. When prompted to save the table, click **Yes**. You should return to **The Earth** database window.

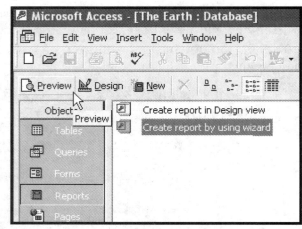

- At **The Earth** database window, click **Reports** under **Objects**.

- Click **Create report by using wizard**.

- Click **Preview**.

- At the first **Report Wizard** dialog box, make sure that **The Highest Mountains** appears in the **Tables/Queries** list box. If it does, you are fine. If it does not, click the **Tables/Queries** list arrow and select **The Highest Mountains** table.

- Under **Available Fields**, click the **Mountain** field to select it.

- Then click the right arrow, so that the **Mountain** field appears under **Selected Fields**.

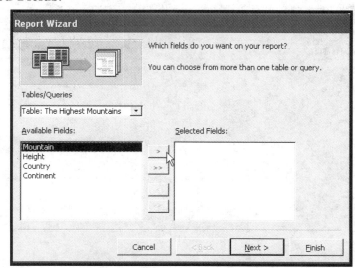

- The second field in the database report will be the Country field, so click the **Country** field to select it.
- Then click the right arrow, so that the **Country** field appears under **Selected Fields**.
- The third field in the database report will be the Height field, so click the **Height** field to select it.

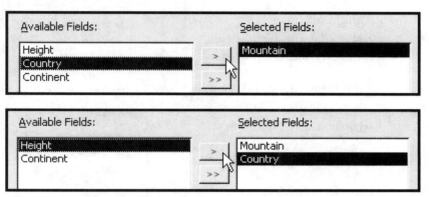

- Then click the right arrow, so that the **Height** field appears under the **Selected Fields**.
- Now that Mountain, Country, and Height are all under Selected Fields, click **Next**. (The Continents field is not part of this report.)

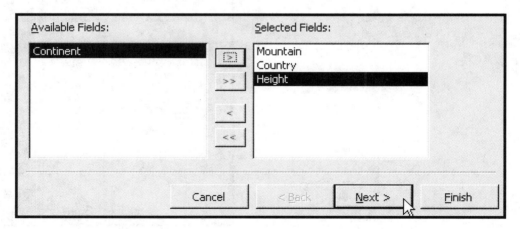

- At the second **Report Wizard** dialog box, simply click **Next**. (There are no grouping levels for this report.)

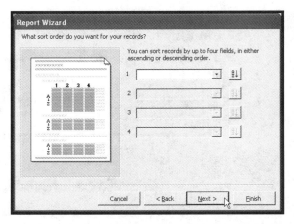

- At the third **Report Wizard** dialog box, simply click **Next**. (You already sorted your database by the Height field. There is no need to sort now.)

- At the fourth **Report Wizard** dialog box, click **Tabular** under **Layout**.

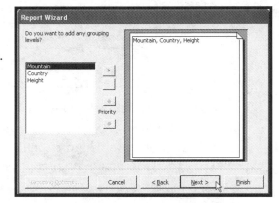

- Click **Portrait** under **Orientation**.

- Then click **Next**.

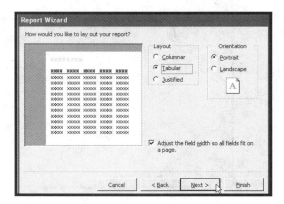

- At the fifth **Report Wizard** dialog box, click **Bold** for the style of the report.

- Then click **Next**.

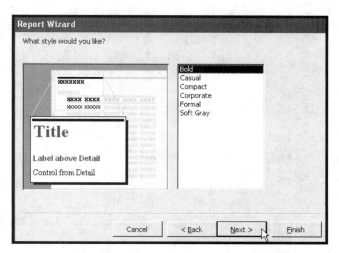

- At the sixth **Report Wizard** dialog box, in the **What title do you want for your report?** text box, make sure that *The Highest Mountains* is displayed. If it is, that's fine. If it is not, click in the text box and type: *The Highest Mountains*

- Make sure that **Preview the Report** is selected under **Do you want to preview the report or modify the report's design?**

- Then click **Finish**.

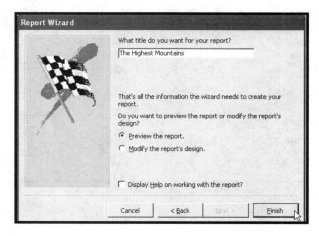

- A preview of the report will appear on your screen. Notice that it is much nicer looking than a printout of the table in Datasheet View.
- To print the report, click the **Print** button on the **Preview** toolbar.

 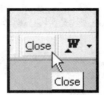

- Then click the **Close** button to return to **The Earth** database window. Notice that **The Highest Mountains** report is now listed and available for you to use whenever you need it.
- Close *The Earth* database file.

The Highest Mountains

Mountain	Country	Height in Feet
Everest	Nepal and Tibet	29,028
Aconcagua	Argentina	22,834
McKinley	United States	20,320
Kilimanjaro	Tanzania	19,340
Elbrus	Russia and Georgia	18,481
Vinson-Massif		16,860
Kosciusko		7,316

Performing Database Queries

You can ask your *Microsoft Access* database a question by performing a database query. Let's say you knew that the population of Alaska was 4,447,100, the population of Hawaii was 1,211,537, and the population of New York was 18,976,457. Soon you began to wonder what the average population of all the states might be. If you have the population of all the states in a *Microsoft Access* database, you can quickly query or ask the database to provide that information—and you will—after a few preliminary steps. First, you will learn how to perform a simple database query using a wizard. Then, you will learn how to perform that same query in Design View. Finally, you will perform a database query in which you ask *Microsoft Access* to calculate the average population of the states. Ready?

- First, move the ***Saluting the States Sample*** database file [filename: **statessam.mdb**] from the CD-ROM to the ***Microsoft Access* Projects** folder on your computer if it is not there already. If you don't remember how to do this, review the directions in the Introduction section.

- While the **Open** dialog box is still displayed, turn off the Read-only feature on the file by right-clicking the file, selecting **Properties**, and deselecting the **Read-only** checkbox. Click **OK**.

- Open the ***Saluting the States*** sample database file that is now in your *Microsoft Access* Projects folder in *Microsoft Access*.

- Let's take a quick look at this database first, so you can see why a simple query can be very helpful.
- At the **statessam** database window, click **Tables** under **Objects**.
- Click the **Saluting the States** table in the **Objects List**.
- Click **Open**.

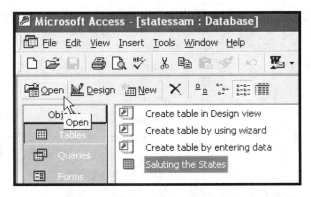

Examine the database. Notice that you can see the State field, but you can't see the Population field. Scroll to the right, and when the Population field comes into view, notice that the State and Abbreviation fields disappear. This can be very bothersome if you want to look up the population data for several states and have to keep scrolling back and forth to obtain the information.

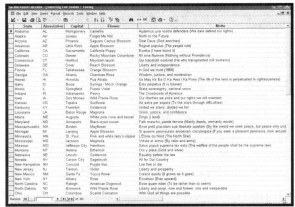

The solution is to place these two fields side-by-side. You can do this by performing a simple query.

Performing a Simple Query Using a Wizard

- Close the **Saluting the States** table. You will return to the **statessam** database window.
- Click **Queries** under **Objects**.
- Click **Create query by using wizard** under the **Objects List**.
- Click **Open**.

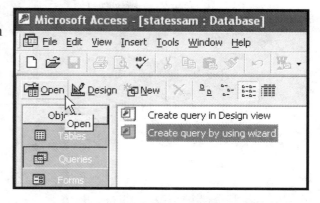

- At the first **Simple Query Wizard** dialog box, click **State** under **Available Fields**.
- Click the right arrow. **State** will move to the right and appear under **Selected Fields**.
- Click **Population** under **Available Fields**.
- Click the right arrow. **Population** will move to the right under **Selected Fields**.
- Click **Next**.

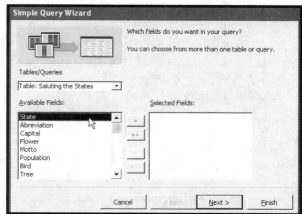

- At the second Simple Query Wizard dialog box, click **Detail (shows every field of every record)**.

- Then click **Next**.

- At the third Simple Query Wizard dialog box, click in the textbox below **What title do you want for your query?**

- Type the following: *Saluting the States Query 1*

- Click **Open the query to view information**.

- Click **Finish**.

- When you return to your database, only the two fields that you selected are displayed.

- Click the **Close** button to close the database query and return to the **statessam** database window.

- Notice that the query you just created is listed as **Saluting the States Query 1** under the **Objects List**.

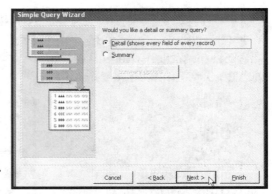

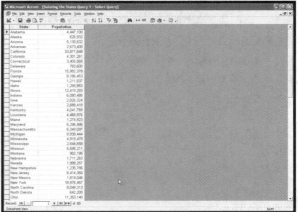

Performing a Simple Query in Design View

You can perform the same simple query in Design view. Ready to try?

- Click **Queries** under **Objects**.
- Click **Create query in Design view**.
- Click **Open**.
- At the **Show Table** dialog box, click the Tables tab to bring it to the forefront if it is not already there.

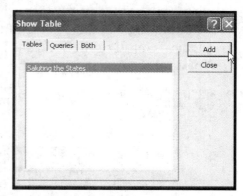

- Click **Saluting the States** if it is not already selected.
- Click **Add**.
- You will see the field list for the *Saluting the States* database appear in the **Select Query** window.

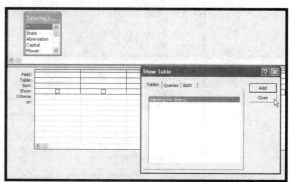

- Click the **Close** button in the Show Table dialog box, so that it is no longer on your screen.

- In the **Field List**, double-click the **State** field.

  When you do, you will see the name of the field—**State**—and the name of the database table—**Saluting the States**—appear in the first pane of the design grid.

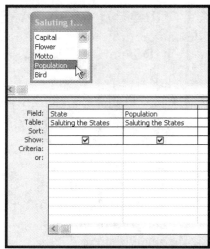

- Then, in the field list, scroll down and double-click the **Population** field.

  You will see the name of the field—**Population**—and the name of the database table—**Saluting the States**—appear in the second pane of the design grid.

- Click **Query** on the **Menu** bar.
- Click **!Run**.

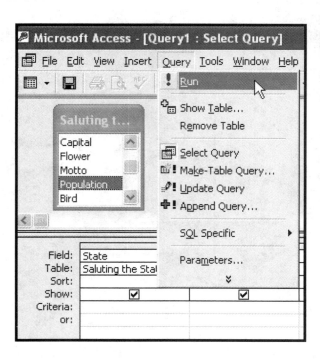

When you do, notice that you created the same simple query in Design view that you did when using a wizard.

Click the **Close** window to return to the **statessam** database window.

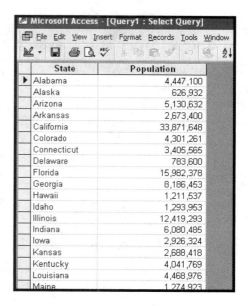

- You will be prompted to save your query. Click **Yes**.
- At the **Save As** dialog box, click in the **Query Name** textbox and type the following: *Saluting the States Query 2*
- Then click **OK**.

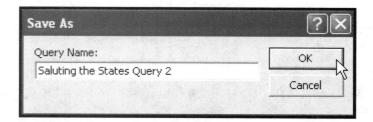

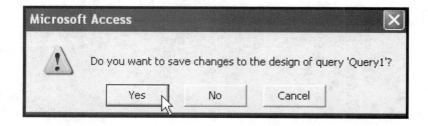

Performing a Query with a Simple Mathematical Calculation

Now that you have two queries under your belt, it's time to add another aspect—a mathematical function, or specifically, an average of the state populations. Eeekkk, you say? Well, it's really not that hard. I promise. Here we go!

- Click **Queries** under **Objects**, if it not already selected.
- Click **Create query in Design view**.
- Click **Open**.
- At the **Show Table** dialog box, click the **Tables** tab to bring it to the forefront, if it is not already there.
- Click **Saluting the States**, if it is not already selected.
- Click **Add**.

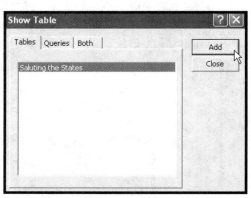

When you do, the field list for the Saluting the States table appears in the Select Query window.

- Then click the **Close** button in the **Show Table** dialog box to remove it from the screen.
- Scroll down the field list and double-click the **Population** field.

- When you do, you will see the name of the field—**Population**—and the name of the database table—**Saluting the States**—appear in the first pane of the design grid.

- Click **View** on the **Menu** bar.

- Click **Totals**.

  When you do, notice that a **Total** row has been added below the Table row in the design grid.

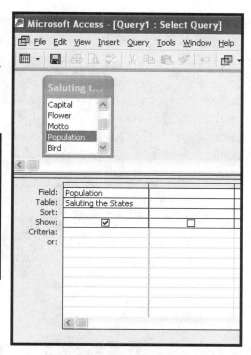

- In the **Total** row click the list arrow to the right of **Group by**.

- Select **Avg** for average.

- Once Avg appears in the Total row, click **Query** on the **Menu** bar.

- Click **!Run**.

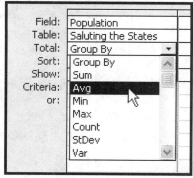

- The average of the Population field will appear on your screen. See, that wasn't so hard!

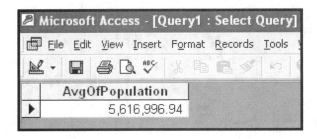

- Click the **Close** button for your query.
- When you are prompted to save your query, click **Yes**.
- When you are prompted to name your query, type the following: *Saluting the States Query 3*
- When you return to the **statessam** database window, notice that you now have three queries under the Objects List.

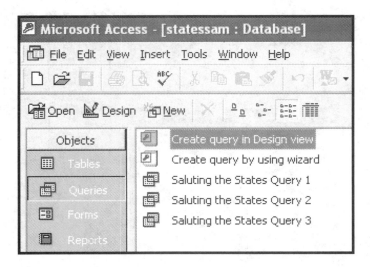

Converting Your Database into a Web Page Document

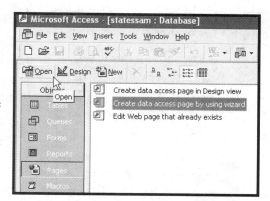

Think of the following scenario: your students have put a lot of work into their research and creating a database. You are proud of what they have accomplished. Now it's time to share your database with the rest of the world via your classroom Web page.

One of the Objects in *Microsoft Access* is Pages. The Pages Object allows you to convert your database into an HTML document. It's actually a very amazing feat because although your database is now an HTML document, it's still functional. Users of your Web page can scroll through the records in your database to view all the research.

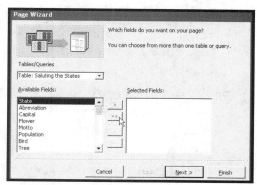

So, now you will use the Pages Object to convert the *Saluting the States* database into an HTML document. Then you'll add a title and view how it functions as a Web page. Here's how:

- Open the ***Saluting the States Sample*** database file from your *Microsoft Access* Projects folder, if it is not already opened [**filename: statessam.mdb**].

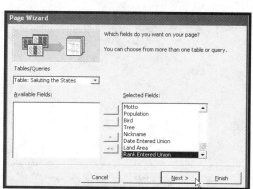

Using the Page Wizard

- Click **Pages** under **Objects**.
- Click **Create data access page by using wizard** under the **Objects List**.
- Click **Open**.
- At the first Page Wizard dialog box, click the double arrow that points to the right between the Available Fields list and the Selected Fields list.

- Once you see all the fields listed under Selected Fields, click **Next**.

- At the second Page Wizard dialog box, simply click **Next**.

- At the third Page Wizard dialog box, simply click **Next**.

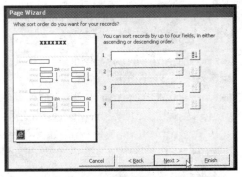

- At the fourth Page Wizard dialog box, click in the textbox below **What title do you want for your page?** and type the following if it is not already there: *Saluting the States*

- Click **Modify the page's design**.

- Then click **Do you want to apply a theme to your page?**

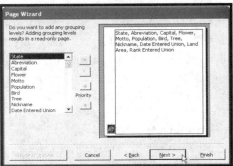

- Finally, click **Finish**.

- At the **Theme** dialog box, click a theme that you like under **Choose a Theme**.

  Special Note: I also clicked **Vivid Colors** and deselected **Background Image**, so that I could have solid colors. It's up to you!

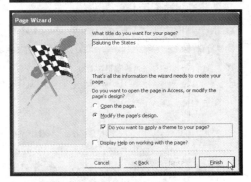

- Then click **OK**.

Adding a Title to the Database Web Page

- At the **Page1: Data Access Page** window, click in the title placeholder and type a title for your database, such as *Ms. Ray's Class Salutes the States*

  Special Note: To create a two-line title, hold the **<Shift>** key down on your keyboard when you press **<Enter>**.

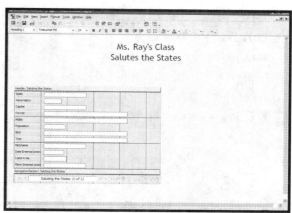

Viewing the Database Web Page

- Click the **View** button on the toolbar to see what your database will look like as a Web Page.

- Yeah! Use the navigation buttons to explore your Web-ready database. All of the data for all of the states are there.

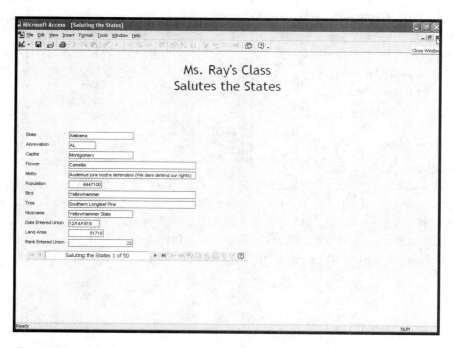

Closing and Saving the Database Web Page

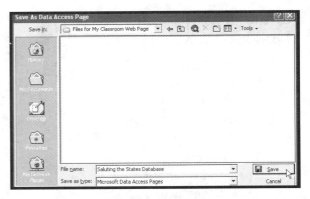

- When you are finished exploring the database, close the Web page:
- Click **File** on the **Menu** bar.
- Click **Close**.

  You will be prompted to save your work. Click **Yes**.

- At the **Save As Data Access Page**, click the **Save in** list arrow and navigate to a folder where you would like to save your database Web page.
- Click in the **Filename** text box and type a name for your database Web page, such as *Saluting the States Database*.
- Click the **Save** button.
- When you return to the database window, you will see your database Web page under the Objects List.

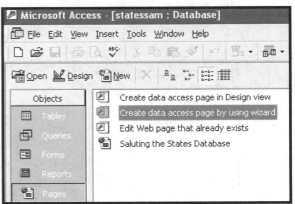

- Close your *Saluting the States* database file.
- Close *Microsoft Access*.

In Conclusion

Congratulations! You have designed and created your own database—even two! You have entered data into your database and modified its design. You have created a database form, learned how to sort your database, and created a database report. You have even learned how to ask questions of and get answers from your database in the form of queries. Now it's time to begin using *Microsoft Access* with your students.

Index of Microsoft Access Student Projects

The Wonder of Whales—A Collection of Poetry

Did you know that the blue whale is the largest animal on this planet? It can grow as large as three railroad cars!

Project Description

Whales are fascinating creatures. It is fun to learn and write about them. In this project, students complete three activities:

1. Students gather data about whales and record the information in a *Microsoft Access* database.

2. Students use this information to write a variety of poems about whales, including cinquain, haiku, quatrain, and limerick poetry.

3. Student poems are illustrated and gathered into a culminating presentation entitled *The Wonders of Whales—A Collection of Poetry*.

Hardware and Software Needed

The following are the hardware and software applications you will need to complete the three project activities:

Gathering Whale Data

For the first activity in this project you will need your computer system and *Microsoft Access*. If you choose to have your students complete their research about whales on the World Wide Web, you will also need access to the Internet.

Writing Whale Poetry

For the second activity in this project, you will need your computer system and a word processing software application, such as *Microsoft Word*.

Creating a Whale Poetry Presentation

For the third activity in this project, you will need your computer system and a presentation software application, such as *Microsoft PowerPoint*. You will also need access to whale clip art or digital photographs. These may be obtained from reference CDs in your classroom or from Web sites.

Special Note: If you have the resources, make available additional computers on which students can work.

CD-ROM Files

The following files are provided to help you and your students complete this project. All the files are available on the CD-ROM found in the back of this book.

Name of File	Description	Software Application	Filename on the CD-ROM
Whales Internet Sites	resource file	*Microsoft Word*	whaleint.doc
Whales	database file	*Microsoft Access*	whales.mdb
Whales (Sample)	sample database file	*Microsoft Access*	whalesam.mdb
A Whale of a Cinquain Poem	student writing prompt template	*Microsoft Word*	cinquain.dot
A Handsome Whale Haiku	student writing prompt template	*Microsoft Word*	haiku.dot
A Cute Whale Quatrain	student writing prompt template	*Microsoft Word*	quatrain.dot
A Laughable Whale Limerick	student writing prompt template	*Microsoft Word*	limerick.dot
The Wonder of Whales—A Collection of Poetry Sample	sample presentation file	*Microsoft PowerPoint*	whalessam.ppt
The Wonder of Whales—A Collection of Poetry Template	presentation file	*Microsoft PowerPoint*	whalestem.ppt
Whales to Research	resource file	*Microsoft Word*	whalesre.doc

Materials Needed and File Preparation

The following are the materials you will need and the files you will need to prepare to complete the three project activities:

Gathering Whale Data

- For this activity, provide students with a variety of books about whales. You will find a list of books related to whales in the **Additional Resources** section of this project.

- You may also wish to bookmark several Web sites related to whales on the computer in your classroom. To help you with this task, open the ***Whales Internet Sites*** resource file that is partially shown on this page. This resource file is available on the CD-ROM [filename: **whaleint.doc**]. It is a four-page *Microsoft Word* document that contains more than 60 hyperlinks to Internet sites about whales. Click a hyperlink and see if you like the site. If you do, bookmark the site for your students.

Whales Internet Sites

Whales: General Sites
- http://www.photolib.noaa.gov/animals/whales1.html
- http://whales.magna.com.au/DISCOVER/gallery/index.html
- http://www.cetacea.org/whales.htm
- http://nmml01.afsc.noaa.gov/education/cetaceans/cetacea.htm
- http://library.thinkquest.org/2605/?tqskip=1

Whales: Specific Sites

Baird's Beaked Whales
- http://mbgnet.mobot.org/salt/whale/baird.htm
- http://library.thinkquest.org/2605/baird.htm
- http://www.montereybaywhalewatch.com/phbairds.htm
- http://animaldiversity.ummz.umich.edu/accounts/berardius/b._bairdii$narrative.html
- http://www.cetacea.org/bairds.htm

Beluga Whales (White Whales)
- http://mbgnet.mobot.org/salt/whale/white.htm
- http://collections.ic.gc.ca/arctic/species/beluga.htm
- http://www.selu.com/bio/wildlife/mammal/whale/beluga01.html
- http://www.speciesatrisk.gc.ca/Species/English/SearchDetail.cf

---

Special note: Web sites can be short-lived. All of these sites are active at the time of this book's publication. However, you may come across a Web page that no longer exists. If you click a link and the Web page cannot be found, try typing a truncated version of the address into the Address box of your browser and pressing <Enter> on your keyboard (for example, the truncated address for http://www.photolib.noaa.gov/animals/whales1.html is http://www.photolib.noaa.gov OR http://www.photolib.noaa.gov/animals). This will take you to the home page or a related page of the same Web site. From there, you can navigate to the Web page you are looking for.

- Create a **Whales Project** folder on the hard disk drive of each computer that will be used to complete this project. By creating this folder on each computer, you and your students will have a place to save all the files related to this project.

Special Note: If the computers that students will be using are connected via a network, locate the shared network drive and create a Whales Project folder there. Once you place all the files needed for this project in this folder, students will be able to access the files from any computer connected to the network. Make sure however, that once students open a file, they save the file on the hard disk drive of their assigned computer or on a floppy disk.

- Send the *Whales* database file that is found on the CD-ROM [**filename: whales.mdb**] to the Whales Project folder on every computer that will be used for this project. Be sure to also turn off the Read-only feature on this file on every computer. Alternatively, if the computers are networked, simply send the *Whales* database file to the Whales Project folder you set up on the shared drive, and turn off the Read-only feature on the file. (If you are not sure how to send the database file to a folder or how to turn off the Read-only feature, see the instructions in the Introduction section.)

Writing Whale Poetry

- For this activity, open each of the following template files from the CD-ROM. Save each file to the Whales Project folder on each computer or save each file to the network.
  - *A Whale of a Cinquain Poem* [filename: **cinquain.dot**]
  - *A Handsome Whale Haiku* [filename: **haiku.dot**]
  - *A Cute Whale Quatrain* [filename: **quatrain.dot**]
  - *A Laughable Whale Limerick* [filename: **limerick.dot**]

Special Note: The template files provide samples of all four types of poetry, explanations of how they are written, and writing prompts. These *Microsoft Word* templates require your students to save their work with new names, so the files remain in their original forms, to be used again and again by students.

Creating a Whale Poetry Presentation

- For this activity, open each of the following presentation files from the CD-ROM. Save each file to the Whales Project folder on each computer or save each file to the network.
  - *The Wonder of Whales Sample* [filename: **Whalessam.ppt**]
  - *The Wonder of Whales—A Collection of Poetry Template* [filename: **whalestem.ppt**]

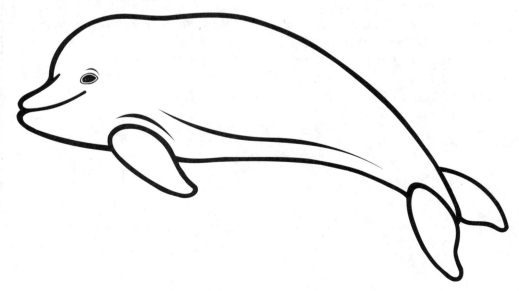

Introducing the Project

Explain to students that they will complete a three-part project:

- First, students will collect data about whales and enter the information they find into a *Microsoft Access* database.
- Second, students will use the information they gathered to write poetry about whales. They will write cinquain, haiku, quatrain, and limerick poems.
- Third, students will create a multimedia presentation of their poetry, entitled *The Wonder of Whales—A Collection of Poetry*, to share with others.

Introducing Gathering Whale Data

First show the students an example of a completed *Whales* database:

- Launch **Microsoft Access**.
- Open the **Whales Sample** database file from the CD-ROM [filename: **whalesam.mdb**].

  Special Note: A dialog box will appear informing you that the database is Read-only. This is fine since you will only be viewing, not changing, this sample database. Click **OK**.

- At the **whalesam** database dialog box, click **Forms** under the **Objects** bar.
- Click **Whale Information** under the **Objects** list.
- Click **Open**.

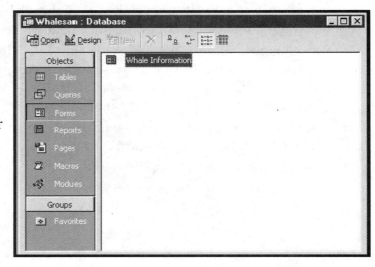

- The *Whale Information* table, displayed in **Form View**, will appear on your screen.

- Explain to students that this is a sample *The Wonder of Whales* form. They will be creating one just like it with information that they gather about a particular type of whale.

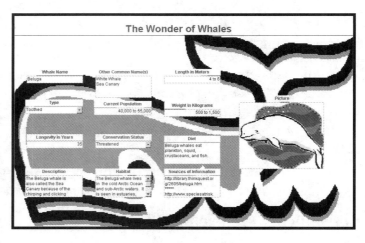

- Explain the features of The Wonder of Whales form as follows:
    - Explain to students that the blue labels are the names of fields in database.
    - Elicit from students the names of the fields they see, such as Whale Name, Other Common Name(s), Length in Meters, Type, Current Population, and more.
    - Explain to students that the white text boxes below the labels are where they will enter information about whales.

- Take a moment to view some of the example data on Beluga whales. Click the list arrows in the Type and Conservation fields. Click in the Description, Habitat, and Sources of Information fields to reveal the scroll bars and to scroll down to see the hidden text.

- Point out the picture of a Beluga whale and explain to the students that they will be entering a picture of a whale in their databases.

- Close the ***Whales Sample*** database file.

Now open and demonstrate to students how to use the *Whales* database file template. Here's how:

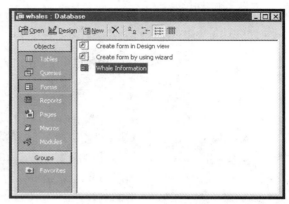

- Open the ***Whales*** database file from your Whales Project folder [filename: **whales.mdb**].

  Special Note: Prior to opening the file, be sure that the Read-only feature is turned off.

- At the **whales** database dialog box, click **Forms** under the **Objects Bar**.

- Click **Whale Information** under the **Objects List**.

- Click **Open**.

- An empty *Whale Information* table, displayed in **Form View,** will appear on your screen.

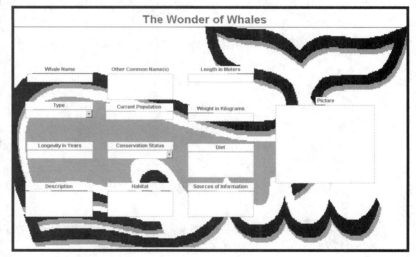

Using the information provided in the instructions below, explain and demonstrate how students should enter data into each field as follows:

- Click in the **Whale Name** field and type the name of your whale, such as *Beluga*. Then press the **<Enter>** key or **<Tab>** key on your keyboard to move to the next field.

- In the **Other Common Name(s)** field, type any other names that your whale is called, such as *White Whale* and *Sea Canary*.

  Special Note: You can type names separated by commas or you can list them as shown in the *Whales Sample* database. If you list them, you must hold down the **<Control>** key on your keyboard as you press **<Enter>** to move to the next line. If you press <Enter> alone, your cursor will jump to the next field.

- In the **Length in Meters** field, type the length of your whale, such as *4 to 6*.

- In the **Type** file, click the list arrow and select **Toothed**.

- In the **Current Population** field, type the number of whales remaining in the oceans, such as *40,000 to 55,000*.

- In the **Weight in Kilograms** field, type the weight of your whale, such as *500 to 1,500*.

- In the **Longevity in Years** field, type the number of years your whale is expected to live, such as *35*.

- In the **Conservation Status** field, click the list arrow and select **Threatened**.

- In the **Diet** field, type the diet of your whale, such as *Beluga whales eat plankton, squid, crustaceans, and fish*.

  Special Note: You can type names separated by commas as shown or you can list them (stacked). If you list them, you must hold down the **<Control>** key on your keyboard as you press **<Enter>** to move to the next line.

- In the **Description** field, type descriptive information about your whale, such as *The Beluga whale is also called the Sea Canary because of the chirping and clicking sounds it makes.*

  Special Note: The text will automatically wrap to the next line and the text box will automatically expand. If you want to start a new paragraph, remember to hold down the **<Control>** key as you press **<Enter>**.

- In the **Habitat** field, type the habitat in which your whale lives, such as *The Beluga whale lives in the cold Arctic Ocean and sub-Arctic waters. It is seen in estuaries, shallow seas, and rivers.*

- In the **Sources of Information** field, enter the sources of the data you find, such as *http://library.thinkquest.org/2605/beluga.htm*

  Special Note: You can copy and paste Web site addresses into this field as well as type the titles and authors of books and other reference material. Insert asterisks between each entry as shown in the *Whales Sample* database. Remember, you must hold down the **<Control>** key as you press **<Enter>** to move to the next line in the text box.

- In the **Picture** field, insert a picture of your whale. Here's how:
  - Click in the picture box to select it.
  - Click **Insert** on the **Menu** bar.
  - Click **Object**.
  - At the **Insert Object** dialog box, you have two options—clicking **Create New** or clicking **Create from File**.
  - If you are going to insert a picture from the *Microsoft Clip Gallery*, click **Create New**.
  - Click **Microsoft Clip Gallery** under **Object Type**.
  - Then click **OK**.

- At the **Microsoft Clip Gallery** dialog box, navigate to the whale picture you want.
- Click the whale picture to select it.
- Then click the **Insert Clip** button.
- The whale picture now appears in the Picture field.

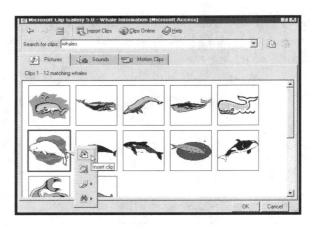

- If you are going to insert a picture from a file that you saved in the Whales Project folder, click **Create from File** in the **Insert Object** dialog box.
- Click the **Browse** button to navigate to the whale picture file.

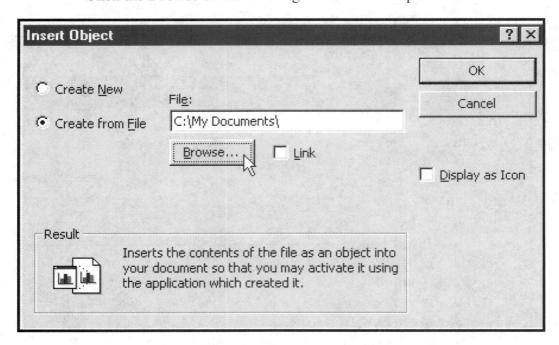

- At the **Browse** dialog box, click the **Look in** list arrow and navigate to the **Whales Project** folder.

- Click the whale picture file you want to select it.

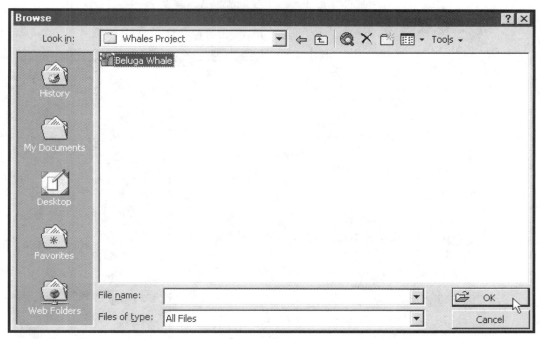

- Click **OK**.
- When you return to the **Insert Object** dialog box, you will see the name of and path to your whale picture file in the **File** textbox. Click **OK**.

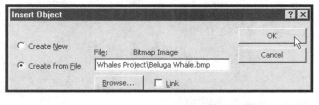

- The whale picture now appears in the Picture field.

- Demonstrate to students how to save the information entered into the *Whales* database by clicking the **Save** button on the Forms toolbar.

- Explain and demonstrate to your students how to use the database navigation buttons in the lower left-hand corner of the screen.

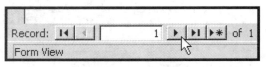

Special Note: Maximize *The Wonder of Whales* form, if necessary, to view the navigation buttons.

Also note that if each student will be working in his or her own database, then there won't be many records to navigate. However, it is still important for them to learn how to use the navigation buttons.

- Explain and demonstrate to your students how to print a single record in a database. Here's how:
- Click **File** on the **Menu** bar.
- Click **Print**.
- At the **Print** dialog box, click **Pages From** under **Print Range**.

Type the number of the record from the database that you want to print in both the **From** and **To** boxes, such as *1* and *1*.

- Click **OK**.

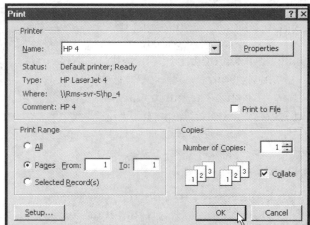

Special Note: Students **should not** use the **Print** button on the **Forms** toolbar. A Print dialog box **will not** appear after clicking this button. The students will not have the opportunity to designate the record(s) they want printed. **All** the records in the database print when clicking the Print button. This may not be an issue if each student is creating his or her own database, but if the students are all working in one database, a lot of unnecessary printing will occur if they click the Print button.

Introducing Writing Whale Poetry and Creating a Whale Poetry Presentation

Open and display *The Wonder of Whales—A Collection of Poetry Sample* presentation file that is shown on the following page [filename: **whalessam.ppt**]. Discuss with students the type and characteristics of the poetry they see about whales. Explain to students that they will be creating their own poems similar to these once their research about whales is complete.

Producing the Project

Assign each student (or have each student select) a whale to research. You will find a list of more than 40 whales to research on page 117. The *Whales to Research* resource file is also available on the CD-ROM [filename: **whalesre.doc**].

Once students complete their research, provide them with the opportunity to enter their findings in the *Whales* database [filename: **whales.mdb**]. (**Special Note:** Make sure that students are opening the *Whales* database from the Whales Project folder on their computers.) Then based upon the information they gathered, have students write their poems about whales. You can use the four student writing prompt template files that are shown on pages 118 and 119. The four student writing prompt template files are:

- *A Whale of a Cinquain Poem* [filename: **cinquain.dot**]
- *A Handsome Whale Haiku* [filename: **haiku.dot**]
- *A Cute Whale Quatrain* [filename: **quatrain.dot**]
- *A Laughable Whale Limerick* [filename: **limerick.dot**]

The Wonder of Whales
A Collection of Poetry

By Ms. Ray's Class

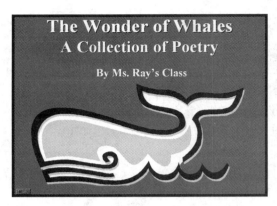

Introduction

Welcome to **The Wonder of Whales**—our collection of poetry about whales. In **The Wonder of Whales** you will find quatrain, limerick, haiku, and cinquain poems about these great ocean creatures. Enjoy!

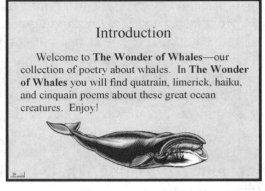

Humpback Whales
by Elizabeth

Humpbacks
Gentle creatures
Swimming, blowing, breaching
Mystically migrate in pods
Whales

Sir Fred, the Beluga Whale
by Anisa

There was a large whale
named Sir Fred.
Who had a huge hump
on his head.
"Please don't tease me!
I'm a Beluga, you see.
Though some call me
'White Whale'
instead."

Gentle Giants
by Noah

Please, deep blue ocean,
Reveal the gentle giants,
Hiding in your waves.

Free the Orcas!
By Corey

Just last night I had the
strangest dream,
That I was finally free.
I swam right through the
Seaquarium—
out of man's captivity.

Whales to Research

Amoux's Beaked Whales
Andrew's Beaked Whales
Bahamonde's Beaked Whales
Baird's Beaked Whales
Beluga Whales
Blainville's Beaked Whales
Blue Whales
Bowhead Whales
Bryde's Whales
Cuvier's Beaked Whales
Dwarf Sperm Whales
False Killer Whales
Fin Whales
Gervais' Beaked Whales
Ginko-Toothed Beaked Whales
Gray Whales
Gray's Beaked Whales
Hector's Beaked Whales
Hubb's Beaked Whales
Humpback Whales
Lesser Beaked Whales

Long-Finned Pilot Whale
Longman's Beaked Whales
Melon-Headed Whales
Minke Whales
Narwhal Whales
Northern Bottlenose Whales
Northern Right Whales
Orca (Killer) Whales
Pygmy Killer Whales
Pygmy Right Whales
Pygmy Sperm Whales
Sei Whales
Shepherd's Beaked Whales
Short-Finned Pilot Whales
Southern Bottlenose Whales
Southern Right Whales
Sowerby's Beaked Whales
Sperm Whales
Straptoothed Whales
True's Beaked Whales

A Whale of a Cinquain Poem

Read the cinquain poem about humpback whales. As you do, notice the following:

- The first line is one word that names the subject of the cinquain poem.
- The second line has two words that describe the subject of the cinquain poem.
- The third line has three verbs that describe the actions of the subject of the cinquain poem.
- The fourth line has four words that express a feeling about the subject of the cinquain poem.
- The fifth line has one word that is a synonym for the subject of the cinquain poem.

Humpbacks
Gentle creatures
Swimming, blowing, breaching
Mystically migrate in pods
Whales

Now, complete a cinquain poem below about the whale that you researched. When you are finished, save this file as instructed by your teacher.

A Laughable Whale Limerick

Read the limerick about a beluga whale named Sir Fred. As you do, notice the following:

- The limerick is humorous.
- The limerick has five lines.
- The limerick has a rhyme scheme of aabba (Fred, head, me, see, instead).
- If you clap as you read the limerick, you will find that lines 1, 2, and 5 have three beats. Lines 3 and 4 have two beats.

Now, complete a limerick below about the whale that you researched. When you are finished, save this file as instructed by your teacher.

There was a large whale named Sir Fred.
Who had a huge hump on his head.
"Please don't tease me!
I'm a Beluga, you see.
Though some call me 'White Whale' instead."

A Handsome Whale Haiku

Read the haiku poem about whales. As you do, notice the following:

- The haiku poem is not rhymed.
- The haiku poem has three lines.
- The haiku poem has seventeen syllables.
- The first line and the third line of the poem have five syllables each.
- The second line of the poem has seven syllables.
- The haiku poem conveys much feeling.

> Please, deep blue ocean,
> Reveal the gentle giants,
> Hiding in your waves.

Now, complete a haiku poem below about the whale that you researched. When you are finished, save this file as instructed by your teacher.

A Cute Whale Quatrain

Read the quatrain poem about an Orca whale in captivity. As you do, notice the following:

- The quatrain poem has four lines.
- The rhyme scheme is abcb. With quatrain poems, you may also use the abab and abba rhyme schemes.

Now, complete a quatrain poem below about the whale that you researched. When you are finished, save this file as instructed by your teacher.

> Just last night I had the strangest dream,
> That I was finally free.
> I swam right through the Seaquarium—
> out of man's captivity.

Have students open the template files, read the sample poems, examine how the poems were created, and then write the first drafts of poems of their own. Students should print their poems and then save their files (with new names) in the Whales Project folder.

Use the writing process with students. Have students edit each other's poems and complete second and third drafts, if necessary.

Once your students' poems are ready for publishing, open *The Wonder of Whales—A Collection of Poetry Template* presentation file [filename: **whalestem.ppt**] from the Whales Project folder. Add your name as the teacher to the title slide.

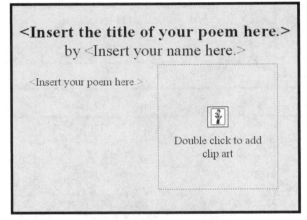

One at a time, have each student copy and paste his or her poem onto a slide within the presentation file. Have each student add a title and byline to his or her slide. Then have each student add a picture illustrating the poem.

Special Note: If students are working at multiple computers, have each student work on their own *The Wonder of Whales—A Collection of Poetry Template* presentation file [filename: **whalestem.ppt**]. Then, assemble all of the students' slides into one presentation by copying and pasting slides into one file.

If your students are adding clip art from the *Microsoft Clip Gallery*, they can simply double-click in the designated clip art area, select the clip art, and click the **Insert Clip** button. If your students are adding pictures from files, they will have to do the following:

- Single-click in the designated clip art area on the slide to select it.
- Click **Insert** on the **Menu** bar.
- Select **Picture**.
- Select **From File**.
- At the **Insert Picture** window, navigate to the folder where the picture file is located.
- Click the picture file to select it.
- Click the **Insert** button.

Your students may have to "work" with their illustrations (e.g., resizing them, moving them, or adding borders). They may also have to format the slide layout and make other design changes to perfect their slides.

Continue using the writing process with students. Have them proofread the slides carefully and make any necessary corrections before sharing *The Wonder of Whales—A Collection of Poetry* with others.

Presenting the Project

Congratulations! Your students collected whale information and entered it into a *Microsoft Access* database. They used this information as a foundation for writing a variety of poems about whales. These poems form *The Wonder of Whales—A Collection of Poetry* presentation that you can share in a number of ways:

- Present *The Wonder of Whales—A Collection of Poetry* to:
  - other classes in your school,
  - your students' parents at an Open House night, or
  - teachers, parents, and others at the next PTSA meeting.
- Publish *The Wonder of Whales—A Collection of Poetry* on your classroom Web site. Then your students' family members and friends across the country (and the world) can view their work.
- Print *The Wonder of Whales—A Collection of Poetry* and bind it for your classroom library.

Additional Project Ideas

Now that students have a wealth of information about whales at their fingertips, have them create a classroom newspaper featuring whales. Include news stories, feature stories, editorials, columns, cartoons, and more—all dedicated to disseminating information about whales. Include topics such as The Magic of Migration, What You Can Do to Save the Whales, When Communication "Clicks," and more.

Additional Resources

Here are a variety of books that provide information about and activities related to whales:

- *Finding Out About Whales* by Elin Kelsey was published in 1998 by Firefly books [ISBN 1895688795].

- *Meeting the Whales: The Equinox Guide to Giants of the Deep* by Erich Hoyt was published in 2000 by Firefly Books [ISBN 0921820232].

- *Whales and Dolphins (Nature Factfile)* by Robin Kerrod was published in 2001 by Southwater Publishers [ISBN 1842154249].

- *Blue* by Michael Hainey was published in 1997 by Penguin USA [ISBN 0201873966].

- *Whales and Other Marine Mammals (Golden Guide)* by George Fichter was published in 1990 by Golden Books Publishing Company [ISBN 0307240754].

- *Humpback Whales* by Francois Gohier was published in 1999 by Econo-Clad Books [ISBN 0785785914].

- *Draw Science Whales, Sharks, and Other Sea Creatures* by Nina Kidd was published in 1999 by Econo-Clad Books [ISBN 0785717870].

- *Whale Tales: Human Interactions with Whales* by Peter Fromm and Andrew Seltser was published in 2000 by Whale Tales Press [ISBN 096487041X].

- *Draw 50 Sharks, Whales, and Other Sea Creatures* by Lee J. Ames and Warren Budd was published in 1989 by Doubleday [ISBN 0385267681].

- *The Whales* by Cynthia Rylant was published in 2000 by Blue Sky Press [ISBN 0590615602].

- *Fun with Whales Stencils* by Paul E. Kennedy was published in 1997 by Dover Publications [ISBN 0486295052].

- *Learning About Whales* by Sy Barlowe and Richard Bonson was published in 1997 by Dover Publications [ISBN 048629787X].

- *Waiting for the Whales* by Sheryl McFarlane was published by Orca Book Publishers [ISBN 0920501966].

- *Whales In the Wild* by Claire Robinson was published in 2001 by Heinemann Library Publications [ISBN 1588103250].

Saluting the United States— Graphically

Project Description

From thirteen original colonies to a nation of 50 states, our country has grown rapidly and prosperously from "sea to shining sea" and beyond. In this project, students complete two activities:

1. Students gather data about the states and record the information in a *Microsoft Access* database.

2. Then students create charts that display the information they gathered about the states.

Hardware and Software Needed

The following are the hardware and software applications you will need to complete the two project activities:

Gathering State Data

For the first activity in this project, you will need your computer system and *Microsoft Access*. If you choose to have your students complete their research for the states on the Web, you will also need access to the Internet.

Creating State Charts

For the second activity in this project, you will need your computer system and a spreadsheet software application, such as *Microsoft Excel*. You will also need a printer—preferably a color printer—to print out the charts your students create.

Special Note: If you have the resources, make available additional computers on which students can work.

CD-ROM Files

The following files are provided to help you and your students complete this project. All the files are available on the CD-ROM found in the back of this book.

Name of File	Description	Software Application	Filename on the CD-ROM
Saluting the States	database file	*Microsoft Access*	states.mdb
State Populations	sample chart	*Microsoft Excel*	statepop.xls
State Sizes	sample chart	*Microsoft Excel*	statesiz.xls
Saluting the States Research Organizer	student research organizer	*Microsoft Word*	statesorg.doc
Fifty States to Research	resource file	*Microsoft Word*	50states.doc
Saluting the States Sample	database file sample	*Microsoft Access*	statessam.mdb
People	clip art file		people.bmp
Scene	clip art file		scene.bmp

Materials Needed and File Preparation

The following are the materials you will need to obtain and the files you will need to prepare to complete the two project activities:

Gathering State Data

- For this activity, provide students with a variety of books about the states. You will find a list of books related to the states in the **Additional Resources** section of this project.

- You may also wish to bookmark several Web sites related to the states on the computer in your classroom. You will find a list of Internet sites related to the states in the **Additional Resources** section of this project.

- Create a **Saluting the States Project** folder on the hard disk drive of each computer that will be used to complete this project. By creating this folder on each computer you and your students will have a place to save all the files related to this project.

  Special Note: If the computers that students will be using are connected via a network, locate the shared network drive and create a Saluting the States Project folder there. Once you place all the files needed for this project in this folder, students will be able to access the files from any computer connected to the network. Make sure however, that once students open a file, they save the file on the hard disk drive of their assigned computer or on a floppy disk.

- Send the *Saluting the States* database file [filename: **states.mdb**] and the *Saluting the States Sample* database file [filename: **statessam.mdb**] that are found on the CD-ROM to the *Saluting the States Project* folder on every computer that will be used for this project. Be sure to also turn off the Read-only feature on both of these files on every computer. Alternatively, if the computers are networked, simply send these *Saluting the States* database files to the *Saluting the States Project* folder you set up on the shared drive, and turn off the Read-only feature on both files. (If you are not sure how to send the database file to a folder or how to turn off the Read-only feature, see the instructions in the Introduction section.)

Creating State Charts

- For this activity, open each of the following spreadsheet files from the CD-ROM. Save each file to the *Saluting the States Project* folder on each computer or save each file to the network.
    - *State Populations* [filename: **statepop.xls**]
    - *State Sizes* [filename: **statesiz.xls**]
- Copy and paste the following clip art files from the CD-ROM to the Saluting the States Project folder on each computer or to the network.
    - *People* [filename: **people.bmp**]
    - *Scene* [filename: **scene.bmp**]

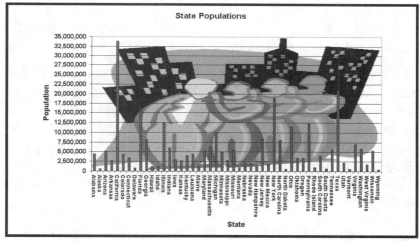

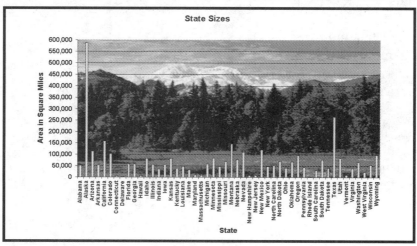

Introducing the Project

Print or open and display the *State Populations* and the *State Sizes* charts
[filenames: **statepop.xls** and **statesiz.xls**] that are shown on the preceding pages.
Have students identify the parts of each chart, such as the title, the horizontal axis
title, the vertical axis title, the category axis, the value axis, and more. Then have
students answer the following questions as they interpret the information
displayed on each chart:

- Which state has the greatest number of people?
- Which state has the fewest number of people?
- Which state is the largest in area?
- Which state is the smallest in area?

Inform students that they will be creating charts similar to these in their **Saluting
the States** project. Explain to students that the *Saluting the States* project
contains two activities:

- First, students will
  collect data about the
  states and enter the
  information they find
  into a *Microsoft Access*
  database. The
  information they will
  gather includes the state
  capitals, two-letter state
  abbreviations, state
  flowers, state mottos,
  state populations, state
  birds, state nicknames,
  state trees, and more.

- Second, students will
  use the information
  they gathered to create
  spreadsheets and then
  charts that display
  information about the
  states.

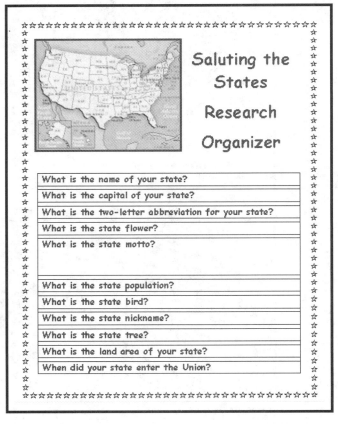

Saluting the States Research Organizer

What is the name of your state?
What is the capital of your state?
What is the two-letter abbreviation for your state?
What is the state flower?
What is the state motto?

What is the state population?
What is the state bird?
What is the state nickname?
What is the state tree?
What is the land area of your state?
When did your state enter the Union?

Provide students with copies of the *Saluting the States Research Organizer* that is shown on the previous page. The ***Saluting the States Research Organizer*** is available on the CD-ROM [filename: **statesorg.doc**]. The research organizer will help students remember and provide a place to record the information they are looking for as they conduct state research.

Special Note: Feel free to add, modify, or delete any of the requested information in the *Saluting the States Research Organizer* to align with your instructional needs and intent.

First show the students an example of a completed *Saluting the States* database:

- Launch ***Microsoft Access***.
- Open the ***Saluting the States Sample*** database file from the CD-ROM [filename: **statessam.mdb**].
- **Special Note:** A dialog box will appear informing you that the database is Read-only. This is fine since you will only be viewing, not changing, this sample database. Click **OK**.
- At the **States** database dialog box, click **Forms** under the **Objects** bar.
- Click **Saluting the States Form** under the **Objects** list.
- Click **Open**.

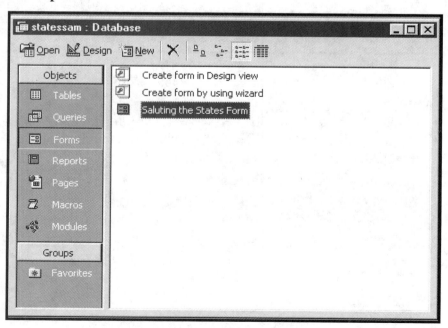

- The **Saluting the States** table, displayed in **Form View**, will appear on your screen.
- Explain to students that this is a sample *Saluting the States* form. They will be creating one just like it with information that they gather about a particular state.

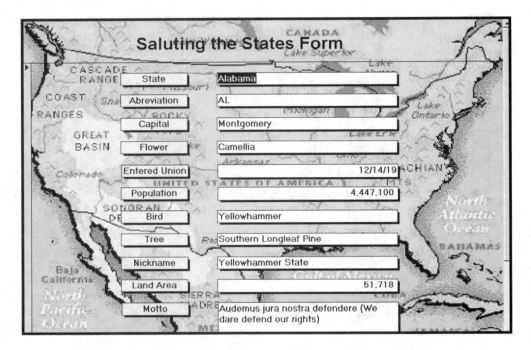

- Explain and demonstrate the features of the *Saluting the States* form as follows:
    - Explain to students that the yellow labels are the names of fields in the database. Elicit from students the names of the fields they see, such as State, Abbreviation, Capital, Flower, and more.
    - Explain to students that the white text boxes next to the labels are where they will enter information about each state.
- Take a moment to view some of the example data on the state of Alabama.
- Close the **Saluting the States Sample** database file.

Now open and demonstrate to students how to use the *Saluting the States* database file template. Here's how:

- Open the **Saluting the States** database file from your *Saluting the States* Project folder [filename: **states.mdb**].

  Special Note: Prior to opening the file, be sure that the Read-only feature is turned off.

- At the **States** database dialog box, click **Forms** under the **Objects** bar.
- Click **Saluting the States Form** under the **Objects** list.

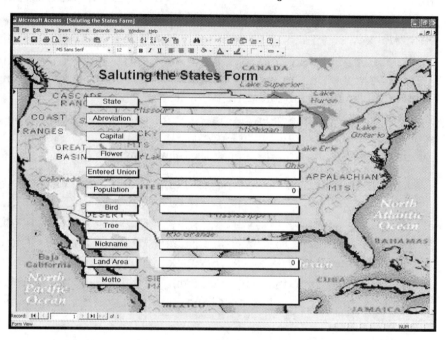

- Click **Open**.
- An empty *Saluting the States* table, displayed in **Form View,** will appear on your screen.

Using the data provided in the instructions below, explain and demonstrate how students should enter data into each field as follows:

- Click in the **State** field and type the name of your state, such as ***Alabama***. Then press the **<Enter>** key or **<Tab>** key on your keyboard to move to the next field.

- In the **Abbreviation** field, type the two-letter abbreviation for the state, such as *AL*. Then press the **<Enter>** key or **<Tab>** key on your keyboard to move to the next field.

- In the **Capital** field, type the capital of the state, such as *Montgomery*. Then press the **<Enter>** key or **<Tab>** key on your keyboard to move to the next field.

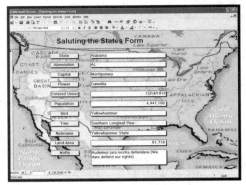

- In the **Flower** field, type the state flower, such *Camellia*. Then press the **<Enter>** key or **<Tab>** key on your keyboard to move to the next field.

- In the **Entered Union** field, type the date the state entered the Union, such as *12/14/1819*. Then press the **<Enter>** key or **<Tab>** key on your keyboard to move to the next field.

Special Note: For the year, be sure to enter all four digits. If you don't type the *18* in *1819*, *Microsoft Access* will automatically assign the number 20, so the birthdate would incorrectly display as 2019.

- In the **Population** field, type the population of the state according to the most recent census, such as *4,447,100*. Then press the **<Enter>** key or **<Tab>** key on your keyboard to move to the next field.

- In the **Bird** field, type the state bird, such as *Yellowhammer*. Then press the **<Enter>** key or **<Tab>** key on your keyboard to move to the next field.

- In the **Tree** field, type the state tree, such as *Southern Longleaf Pine*. Then press the **<Enter>** key or **<Tab>** key on your keyboard to move to the next field.

- In the **Nickname** field, type the nickname of the state, such as the *Yellowhammer State*. Then press the **<Enter>** key or **<Tab>** key on your keyboard to move to the next field.

- In the **Land Area** field, type the area of the state in square miles, such as *51,718*. Then press the **<Enter>** key or **<Tab>** key on your keyboard to move to the next field.

- In the **Motto** field, type the state motto, such as *Audemus jura nostra defendere (We dare defend our rights)*. Then press the **<Enter>** key or **<Tab>** key on your keyboard to move to the next field.

- Demonstrate to students how to save the information entered into the *Saluting the States* database by clicking the **Save** button on the **Forms** toolbar.

- Explain and demonstrate to your students how to use the database navigation buttons in the lower left-hand corner of the screen.

  Special Note: Maximize the *Saluting the States* Form, if necessary, to view the navigation buttons.

- Also note that if each student will be working in his or her own database, then there won't be many records to navigate. However, it is still important for them to learn how to use the navigation buttons.

- Explain and demonstrate to your students how to print a single record in a database.

  - Click **File** on the **Menu** bar.
  - Click **Print**.
  - At the **Print** dialog box, click **Pages From** under **Print Range**.
  - Type the number of the record from the database that you want to print in both the **From** and **To** boxes, such as *1* and *1*.
  - Click **OK**.

Special Note: Students **should not** use the **Print** button on the **Forms** toolbar. A Print dialog box **will not** appear after clicking this button. The students will not have the opportunity to designate the record(s) they want printed. **All** the records in the database print when clicking the Print button. This may not be an issue if each student is creating his or her own database, but if the students are all working in one database, a lot of unnecessary printing will occur if they click the Print button.

Producing the Project

Assign each student (or have each student select) a state to research. You will find a list of the fifty states to research below. The *Fifty States to Research* resource file is also available on the CD-ROM [filename: **50states.doc**].

Once students complete their research, provide them with the opportunity to enter their findings into the *Saluting the States* database. Be sure students understand how to find the database on the computer system, open the database, navigate the database, enter their information, save their work, and close the database.

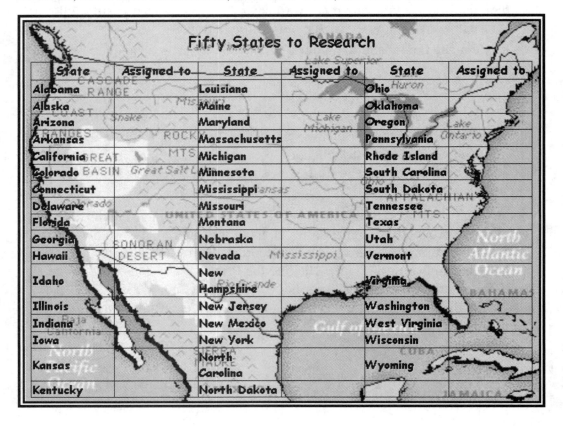

Fifty States to Research

State	Assigned to	State	Assigned to	State	Assigned to
Alabama		Louisiana		Ohio	
Alaska		Maine		Oklahoma	
Arizona		Maryland		Oregon	
Arkansas		Massachusetts		Pennsylvania	
California		Michigan		Rhode Island	
Colorado		Minnesota		South Carolina	
Connecticut		Mississippi		South Dakota	
Delaware		Missouri		Tennessee	
Florida		Montana		Texas	
Georgia		Nebraska		Utah	
Hawaii		Nevada		Vermont	
Idaho		New Hampshire		Virginia	
Illinois		New Jersey		Washington	
Indiana		New Mexico		West Virginia	
Iowa		New York		Wisconsin	
Kansas		North Carolina		Wyoming	
Kentucky		North Dakota			

Once students complete their data entry, create charts that display their research findings. Here's how:

- Open the class' ***Saluting the States*** database file.

  Special Note: If you are having all the students enter their data into one database, then you will open the completed class *Saluting the States* database file. If each student has created his or her own database, then use the ***Saluting the States Sample*** file [filename: **statessam.mdb**]. For the purposes of demonstration, we are using the *Saluting the States Sample* database file that is already populated.

- At the **States** database dialog box, click **Tables** under the **Objects** bar.

- Click **Saluting the States** under the **Objects List**.

- Click **Open**.

- The **Saluting the States** table, displayed in **Datasheet View**, will appear on your screen.

- Click **File** on the **Menu** bar.

- Click **Export**.

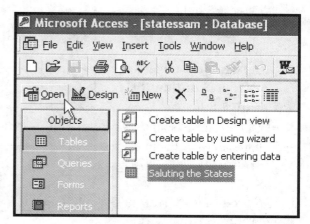

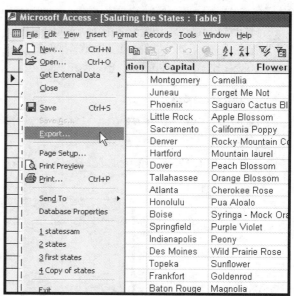

- At the **Export Table** dialog box, click the **Save in** list arrow and navigate to the folder where you want to save the exported table, such as your **Saluting the States** folder.

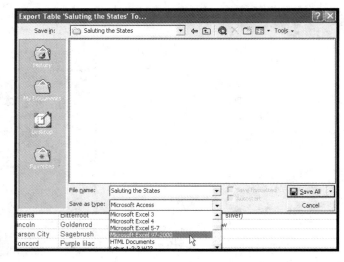

- Click the **Save as type** list arrow and select *Microsoft Excel 97-2000*.

  Special Note: If you prefer to work with another spreadsheet application, feel free to select that application from the list. You will then need to modify the remaining instructions for opening the spreadsheet application and creating a chart to align with the processes used by the selected program.

- Click **Save All**.
- Close your *Saluting the States* database file and *Microsoft Access*.
- Launch *Microsoft Excel*.
- Click the **Open** button on the **Standard** toolbar.

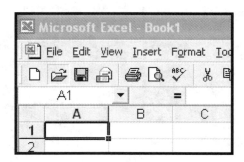

- At the **Open** dialog box, click the **Look in** list arrow and navigate to the folder where you saved the exported **Saluting the States** table.

- Click the **Saluting the States** table to select it.
- Click **Open**.
- The **Saluting the States** data will appear on your screen.
- Click on **Heading A** to select the **State** column for charting.

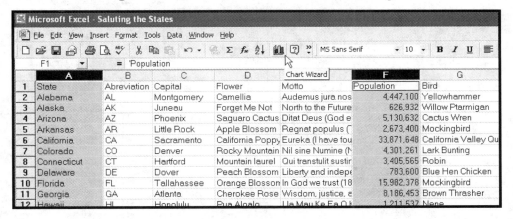

- Hold down the **<Control>** key on your keyboard and click **Heading F** to select the **Population** column for charting.

  Special Note: Holding down the **<Control>** key allows you to select multiple non-adjacent columns.

- Then click the **Chart Wizard** button on the **Standard** toolbar.

- At the **Chart Wizard—Step 1 of 4—Chart Type** dialog box, click **Column** under **Chart type**.

- Click the first chart—**Clustered Column**—under **Chart sub-type**.

- Click **Next**.

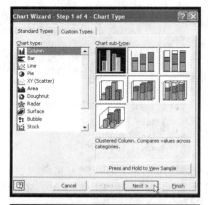

- At the **Chart Wizard—Step 2 of 4—Chart Source Data** dialog box, click **Next**.

- At the **Chart Wizard—Step 3 of 4—Chart Options** dialog box, click the **Titles** tab to bring it to the forefront if it is not already.

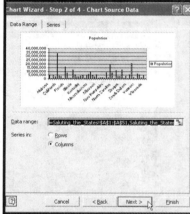

- Click in the **Chart title** text box and type the following: *State Populations*

- Click in the **Category (X) axis** text box and type the following: *State*

- Click in the **Value (Y) axis** text box and type the following: *Population*

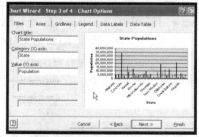

- Click the **Legend** tab to bring it to the forefront.

- Click the **Show legend** box to deselect it and remove the legend from the chart.

- Then click the **Next** button.

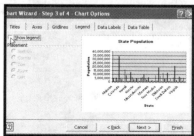

- At the **Chart Wizard—Step 4 of 4—Chart Location** dialog box, click **As new sheet** under **Place Chart**.

- Type the following in the **As new sheet** text box: *State Populations*

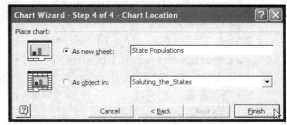

- Click **Finish**.

- The **State Populations** chart will appear on your screen.

Congratulations! You have just created a chart using data imported from a *Microsoft Access* database.

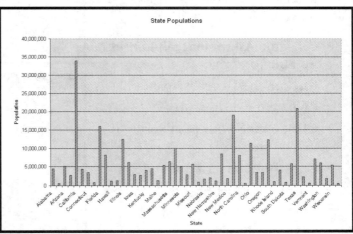

- Now it is time for some finishing touches. Ready to tackle the formatting of your **State Populations** chart? Thought so!

- Double-click anywhere in the **Category Axis** area.

  Special Note: The **Category Axis** area is where you see the names of the states listed.

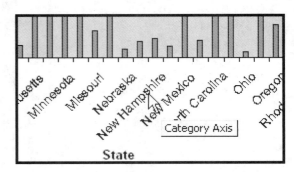

- At the **Format Axis** dialog box, click the **Scale** tab to bring it to the forefront.
- Click in the **Number of categories between tick-mark labels**, remove the number **2**, and type the number *1*.

  Special Note: This will allow the name of each state to be displayed on your chart.

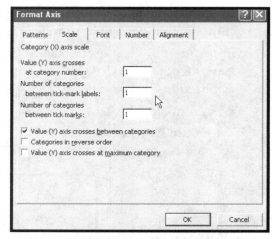

- Click the **Alignment** tab to bring it to the forefront.
- Click in the **Degrees** textbox.
- Change the degrees to *–90*.
- Click on the **Font** tab to bring it to the forefront.
- Click **Bold** under **Font style**.
- Change the font **Size** to **12** points.
- Click **OK** to return to the chart and view the changes you made.

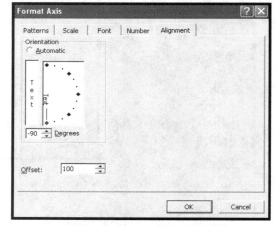

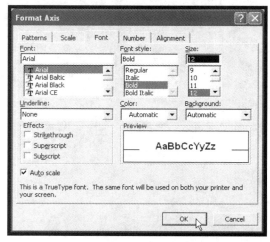

- Double-click the **State** axis title at the bottom of the screen.
- At the **Format Axis Title** dialog box, click the **Font** tab to bring it to the forefront.
- Click **Bold** under **Font style**.
- Change the font **Size** to **14** points.
- Click **OK** to return to the chart and view the changes you made.

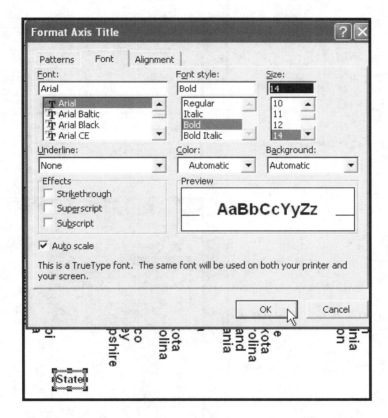

- Now change the **Population** axis title to **Bold** and **14**-point font size.
- Double-click anywhere in the **Value Axis** area.

  Special Note: The **Value Axis** area is where you see the population values listed.

- At the **Format Axis** dialog box, click the **Scale** tab to bring it to the forefront.

- Change the **Maximum** to **35,000,000**.

- Change the **Major unit** to **2,500,000**.

- Click the **Font** tab to bring it to the forefront.

- Click **Bold** under **Font style**.

- Change the font **Size** to **14** points.

- Click **OK** to return to the chart and view the changes you made.

- Double-click the **State Populations** chart title at the top of the screen.

- Click the **Font** tab to bring it to the forefront.

- Click **Bold** under **Font style**.

- Change the font **Size** to **16** points.

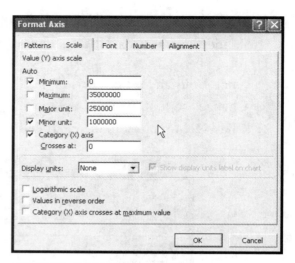

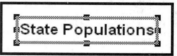

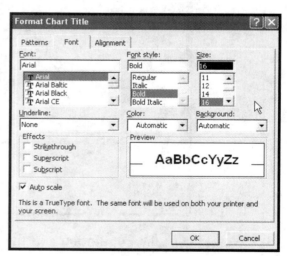

Click **OK** to return to the chart and view the changes
you made.

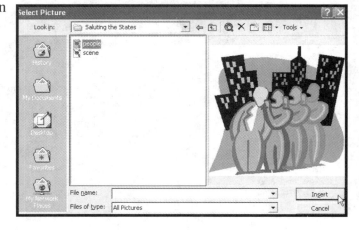

- Double-click in the gray **Plot Area** on your chart.
- **Special Note:** Be careful not to click a grid line.
  Be sure to double-click the gray background area.
- At the **Format Plot Area** dialog box, click **Fill
  Effects**.
- At the **Fill Effects** dialog box, click the **Picture**
  tab to bring it to the forefront.
- Click **Select Picture**.
- At the **Select Picture** dialog box, click the **Look in** list arrow and navigate
  to the folder where you have a picture that would be appropriate for this
  chart, such as a picture of people.

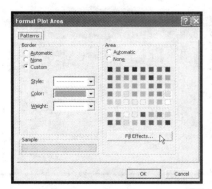 

Special Note: You can
use the picture of
people [filename:
people.bmp] that you
moved into your
Saluting the States
project folder earlier.

- Click the picture to
  select it.
- Click **Insert**.

- When you return to the **Fill Effects** dialog box, click **OK**.
- When you return to the **Format Plot Area** dialog box, click **OK**.
- When you return to your chart, you will see the picture you selected in the plot area, behind the data columns.
- To change the color of the data columns so that they stand out against the picture in the plot area, double-click any one of the data columns.

  Special Note: Make sure that all the data columns are selected, not just one.

- At the **Format Data Series** dialog box, click the **Patterns** tab to bring it to the forefront, if it is not already there.
- Click on a color under **Area**, such as red, that will display clearly on top of the picture.
- Click **OK**.

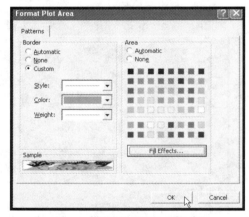

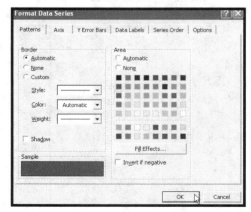

- When you return to your chart, you're done!

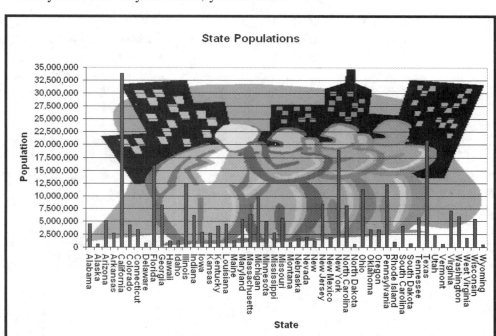

- Now try creating another chart, using the steps previously provided!

  Special Note: The **scene.bmp** file that you moved to the *Saluting the States Project* folder can also be used with the second chart that you create.

Presenting the Project

Congratulations! Your students collected state information and entered it into a *Microsoft Access* database. They used this information as a foundation for creating charts about the states. You can share the charts in a number of ways:

- Create a States bulletin board. Place a large map of the United States in the center of the bulletin board. Print the *State Populations* chart and other charts you created and place them around the map of the United States.

- Publish the *Saluting the States* database and charts on your classroom Web site. Then your students' family members and friends across the country (and the world) can view their work. Plus, the database and charts will be a great resource for other classrooms that are studying the states.

Additional Project Ideas

Now that students have a wealth of information at their fingertips about the 50 states, have them create a multimedia presentation, such as **Guess Which State I Am** that is partially shown on the following page. In this presentation, each student creates two slides about his or her state. The first slide provides clues as to the identity of the state. The second slide provides the state name and a state map. (Maps for every state are available in the *Microsoft Clip Gallery*.)

Special Note: You will find complete step-by-step instructions, a sample presentation file, and a template file for creating this project in *Microsoft PowerPoint Simple Projects (Primary)* published by Teacher Created Materials. Visit Teacher Created Materials on the Internet at http://www.teachercreated.com to view sample pages and to learn how you can order this book.

Additional Resources

The following Internet sites and books will provide you with additional information and educational materials related to the 50 states:

Internet Sites

- Visit the **US50** site to view fact sheets designed to aid research about the fifty United States. Fact sheets include the state populations, state trees, state birds, state nicknames, and more. The Internet site address is:

  http://www.theus50.com/fastfacts.asp

- Visit the **States and Capitals** site to view more than fifty categories of information about the states, such as topography, climate, national parks and forests, historic landmarks, highest and lowest points, governor and representatives, license plates, and maps. The Internet site address is:

  http://www.50states.com/

- Visit the **Global** site to find links to the home pages of all fifty states. The Internet site address is:

  http://www.globalcomputing.com/states.html

- Visit the **Internet Public Library—Stately Knowledge—Facts About the United States** site. You will find an index that provides links to the basic facts about each state. You will also find several charts that address the United States as whole, including the dates each state entered the Union. The Internet site address is:

  http://www.ipl.org/youth/stateknow/

- Visit the **Fifty Nifty United States** site. This ThinkQuest site includes fun information about each state, such as the state insect, the state song, the state stone, and more. The Internet site address is:

  http://www.henry.k12.ga.us/pges/kid-pages/nifty-fifty/default.html

- Visit the **ProTeacher! Fifty United States** site. You will find lesson plans, maps, worksheets, and other classroom materials related to each state. The Internet site address is:

  http://www.proteacher.com/090082.shtml

- Visit the **Teacher Vision** site for **Fifty Fun Facts About the United States**. At this site, you will also find a Lesson Planning Center, Teacher Tools, and more. The Internet site address is:

  http://www.teachervision.com/lesson-plans/lesson-684.html

Books

- *The Amazing 50 States Maze Book* by Scott Sullivan was published in 2001 by Price Stein Sloan Publishers [ISBN 0843176563].
- *Fabulous Facts About the 50 States* by Wilma Ross was published in 1991 by Scholastic Paperbacks [ISBN 0590448862].
- *Celebrate the 50 States!* by Loreen Leedy was published in 1999 by Holiday House [ISBN 0823414310].
- *The United States of America—A State-by-State Guide* by Millie Miller was published in 1999 by Scholastic Trade [ISBN 0590043749].
- *Kids Learn America! Bringing Geography to Life with People, Places, and History* by Patricia Gordon was published in 1999 by Williamson Publishing [ISBN 1885593317].
- *Celebrate the States* (5-book set) by the American Library Association was published by Benchmark Books in 2000 [ISBN 0761410619].

Presidential Portraits

Project Description

In 2001 George W. Bush was elected the 43rd president of the United States. We know a lot about our current president—like his age, the state he came from, his political party, and more. But what about the other 42 presidents that have served our country? In this project students learn about the presidents of the United States, while completing two activities:

First, students gather data about the presidents of the United States and record the information in a *Microsoft Access* database.

Second, students create presidential portraits using cereal boxes. Students cover the boxes with construction paper and then cover them with information they have gathered about their presidents.

Hardware and Software Needed

The following are the hardware and software applications you will need to complete the three project activities:

Gathering Presidential Data

For the first activity in this project, you will need your computer system and *Microsoft Access*. If you choose to have your students complete their research for the presidents on the Web, you will also need access to the Internet.

Creating Presidential Portraits

For the second activity in this project, you will need your computer system and word processing software, such as *Microsoft Word*. Having a word processing program available will give your students the option of creating components of the Presidential Portraits by hand or on the computer.

Special Note: If you have the resources, make available additional computers on which students can work.

CD-ROM Files

The following files are provided to help you and your students complete this project. All the files are available on the CD-ROM found in the back of this book.

Name of File	Description	Software Application	Filename on the CD-ROM
The Presidents	database file	*Microsoft Access*	pres1.mdb
The Presidents Sample	sample database file	*Microsoft Access*	pressam.mdb
How to Make a Presidential Portrait	presentation file	*Microsoft PowerPoint*	pres2.ppt
Presidents to Research	resource file	*Microsoft Word*	pres3.doc
Presidential Portrait Checklist and Score Sheet	organizer and score sheet file	*Microsoft Word*	pres4.doc

Materials Needed and File Preparation

The following are the materials you will need to obtain and the files you will need to prepare to complete the two project activities:

Gathering Presidential Data

For this activity, provide students with a variety of books about the presidents. You will find a list of books related to the presidents in the **Additional Resources** section of this project.

- You may also wish to bookmark several Web sites related to the presidents on the computer in your classroom. You will find a list of Internet sites related to the presidents in the **Additional Resources** section of this project.

- Create a **Presidents Project** folder on the hard disk drive of each computer that will be used to complete this project. By creating this folder on each computer you and your students will have a place to save all of the files related to this project.

  Special Note: If the computers that students will be using are connected via a network, locate the shared network drive and create a Presidents Project folder there. Once you place all the files needed for this project in this folder, students will be able to access the files from any computer connected to the network. Make sure however, that once students open a file, they save the file on the hard disk drive of their assigned computer or on a floppy disk.

- Send *The Presidents* database file [filename: **pres1.mdb**] that is found on the CD-ROM to the Presidents Project folder on every computer that will be used for this project. Be sure to also turn off the Read-only feature of this file on every computer. Alternatively, if the computers are networked, simply send the *Presidents* database file to the Presidents Project folder you set up on the shared drive, and turn off the Read-only feature on the file. (If you are not sure how to send the database file to a folder or how to turn off the Read-only feature, see the instructions in the Introduction section.)

Creating a Presidential Portrait

- For this activity, open the *How to Create a Presidential Portrait* presentation file from the CD-ROM [filename: **pres2.ppt**]. Save this file to the Presidents Project folder on your computer or save the file to the network.

- Make copies of the *Presidential Portrait Checklist and Score Sheet* that is displayed on the last page of this project. You can copy this page from the book or open and print the file from the CD-ROM [filename: **pres4.doc**].

Introducing the Project

Explain to students that they will complete a two-part project about the presidents:

- First, students will collect data about the presidents and enter the information they find into a *Microsoft Access* database. The information they will need includes the names of the presidents, the dates they were born, the locations where they were born, and more. Students may also enter pictures related to the presidents.

- Second, students will use the information they gathered to create Presidential Portraits. Then they will share these portraits with others.

First show the students an example of a completed *The Presidents* database:

- Launch **Microsoft Access**.

- Open **The Presidents Sample** database file from the CD-ROM [filename: **pressam.mdb**].

  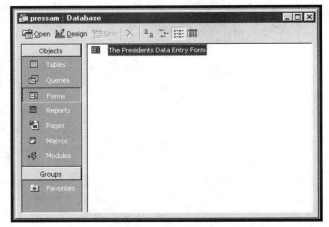

  Special Note: A dialog box will appear informing you that the database is Read-only. This is fine since you will only be viewing, not changing, this sample database. Click **OK**.

- At the **pressam** database dialog box, click **Forms** under the **Objects Bar**.
- Click **The Presidents Data Entry Form** under the **Objects** list.
- Click **Open**.

- The Presidents Sample table, displayed in **Form View**, will appear on your screen.

- Explain to students that this is a sample The Presidents Data Entry Form. They will be creating one just like it with information that they gather about a particular president.

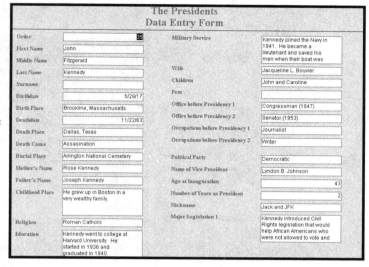

- Explain and demonstrate the features of The Presidents Data Entry Form as follows:

  - Explain to students that the words in brown are the names of the fields in *The Presidents* database. Elicit from students the names of the fields they see, such as Order, First Name, Middle Name, Last Name, Surname, Birthdate, and more.

    Special Note: This form has additional fields that may be viewed if you scroll to the right.

  - Explain to students that the white text boxes next to the labels are where they will enter information about the presidents.

- Take a moment to view some of the example data on President Kennedy.

- Close **The Presidents** database file.

Now open and demonstrate to students how to use *The Presidents* database file template. Here's how:

- Open *The Presidents* database file from your Presidents Project folder [filename: **pres1.mdb**].

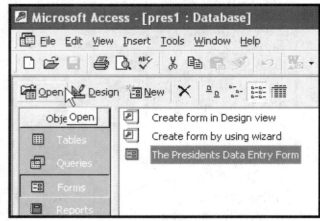

  Special Note: Prior to opening the file, be sure that the Read-only feature is turned off.

- At the **pres1** database dialog box, click **Forms** under the **Objects Bar**.

- Click **The Presidents Data Entry Form** under the **Objects List**.

- Click **Open**.

- An empty The Presidents table, displayed in **Form View,** will appear on your screen.

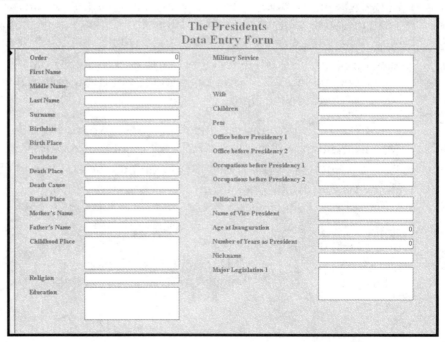

Using the data provided in the instructions below, explain and demonstrate how students should enter data into each field as follows:

- Click in the **Order** field and type the number that represents the numerical order of your president, such as *35* (for the 35th president). Then press the **<Enter>** key or **<Tab>** key on your keyboard to move to the next field.

- In the **First Name** field, type the first name of your president, such as *John*. Then press the **<Enter>** key or **<Tab>** key on your keyboard to move to the next field.

- In the **Middle Name** field, type the middle name of your president, such as *Fitzgerald*. Then press the **<Enter>** key or **<Tab>** key on your keyboard to move to the next field.

- In the **Last Name** field, type the last name of your president, such as *Kennedy*. Then press the **<Enter>** key or **<Tab>** key on your keyboard to move to the next field.

- In the **Surname** field, type any surname that your president has, such as *Jr.* Then press the **<Enter>** key or **<Tab>** key on your keyboard to move to the next field.

- In the **Birthdate** field, type your president's birth date, such as *5/29/1917*. Then press the **<Enter>** key or **<Tab>** key on your keyboard to move to the next field.

  Special Note: For the year, be sure to enter all four digits. If you don't type the *19* in *1917*, *Microsoft Access* will automatically assign the number 20, so the birthdate would incorrectly be entered as 2017.

- In the **Birth Place** field, type the location where your president was born, such as *Brookline, Massachusetts*. Then press the **<Enter>** key or **<Tab>** key on your keyboard to move to the next field.

- In the **Deathdate** field, type the day that your president died if he is no longer alive, such as *11/22/1963*. Then press the **<Enter>** key or **<Tab>** key on your keyboard to move to the next field.

- In the **Death Place** field, type the location where your president died if he is no longer alive, such as *Dallas, Texas*. Then press the **<Enter>** key or **<Tab>** key on your keyboard to move to the next field.

- In the **Death Cause** field, type the cause of your president's death if he is no longer alive, such as *Assassination*. Then press the **<Enter>** key or **<Tab>** key on your keyboard to move to the next field.

- In the **Burial Place** field, type where your president's body is buried if he is no longer alive, such as *Arlington National Cemetery*. Then press the **<Enter>** key or **<Tab>** key on your keyboard to move to the next field.

- In the **Mother's Name** field, type the name of your president's mother, such as *Rose Kennedy*. Then press the **<Enter>** key or **<Tab>** key on your keyboard to move to the next field.

- In the **Father's Name** field, type the name of your president's father, such as *Joseph Kennedy*. Then press the **<Enter>** key or **<Tab>** key on your keyboard to move to the next field.

- In the **Childhood Place** field, explain where your president grew up, such as *He grew up in Boston in a very wealthy family*. Then press the **<Enter>** key or **<Tab>** key on your keyboard to move to the next field.

- In the **Religion** field, type the name of your president's faith, such as *Roman Catholic*. Then press the **<Enter>** key or **<Tab>** key on your keyboard to move to the next field.

- In the **Education** field, explain your president's education, such as *Kennedy went to college at Harvard University*. Then press the **<Enter>** key or **<Tab>** key on your keyboard to move to the next field.

- In the **Military Service** field, explain your president's military service if he was in the armed forces, such as *Kennedy joined the Navy in 1941*. Then press the **<Enter>** key or **<Tab>** key on your keyboard to move to the next field.

- In the **Wife** field, type the name of your president's wife, such as *Jacqueline L. Bouvier*. Then press the **<Enter>** key or **<Tab>** key on your keyboard to move to the next field.

- In the **Children** field, type the name or names of your president's children, such as *John and Caroline*. Then press the **<Enter>** key or **<Tab>** key on your keyboard to move to the next field.

- In the **Pets** field, type the name or names of your president's pets if he had them while in the White House. For Kennedy, no mention of pets could be found, so leave this field blank. Then press the <**Enter**> key or <**Tab**> key on your keyboard to move to the next field.

- In the **Office before Presidency 1** field, type the name of political office that your president held before becoming the President, such as *Congressman (1947)*. Then press the <**Enter**> key or <**Tab**> key on your keyboard to move to the next field.

- In the **Office before Presidency 2** field, type the name of a second political office that your president held before becoming the President, such as *Senator (1953)*. Then press the <**Enter**> key or <**Tab**> key on your keyboard to move to the next field.

- In the **Occupations before Presidency 1** field, type the name of one occupation that your president held before becoming the President, such as *Journalist*. Then press the <**Enter**> key or <**Tab**> key on your keyboard to move to the next field.

- In the **Occupations before Presidency 2** field, type the name of a second occupation that your president held before becoming the president, such as *Writer*. Then press the <**Enter**> key or <**Tab**> key on your keyboard to move to the next field.

- In the **Political Party** field, type the name of your president's political party, such as *Democratic*. Then press the <**Enter**> key or <**Tab**> key on your keyboard to move to the next field.

- In the **Name of Vice President** field, type the name of the vice president who served during your president's term(s) in office, such as *Lyndon B. Johnson*. Then press the <**Enter**> key or <**Tab**> key on your keyboard to move to the next field.

- In the **Age at Inauguration** field, type how old your president was when he took his oath of office, such as *43*. Then press the **<Enter>** key or **<Tab>** key on your keyboard to move to the next field.

- In the **Number of Years as President** field, type the number of years your president held his office, such as *2*. Then press the **<Enter>** key or **<Tab>** key on your keyboard to move to the next field.

- In the **Nickname** field, type any nicknames that your president was called, such as *Jack and JFK*. Then press the **<Enter>** key or **<Tab>** key on your keyboard to move to the next field.

- In the **Major Legislation 1** field, explain any major legislation that your president introduced during his term in office, such as ***Kennedy introduced Civil Rights legislation that would help African Americans who were not allowed to vote and were segregated from society***. Then press the **<Enter>** key or **<Tab>** key on your keyboard to move to the next field.

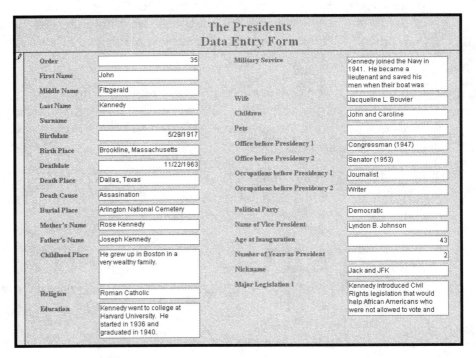

- Scroll to the right to view the **Major Legislation 2** field, as well as the remaining fields in *The Presidents* database.

Major Legislation 2	
Major Accomplishments 1	
Major Accomplishments 2	
Major World Events 1	
Major World Events 2	
Other Notes 1	
Other Notes 2	

Picture

- In the **Major Legislation 2** field, explain any other major legislation that your president introduced during his term in office, such as *Kennedy introduced the New Frontier legislation that would stimulate the nation's economy*. Then press the **<Enter>** key or **<Tab>** key on your keyboard to move to the next field.

- In the **Major Accomplishments 1** field, explain a major accomplishment of your president, such as *He formed the Alliance for Progress and the Peace Corps*. Then press the **<Enter>** key or **<Tab>** key on your keyboard to move to the next field.

- In the **Major Accomplishments 2** field, explain a second major accomplishment of your president, such as *Kennedy wrote a Pulitzer Prize-winning book entitled Profiles in Courage*. Then press the **<Enter>** key or **<Tab>** key on your keyboard to move to the next field.

- In the **Major World Events 1** field, explain a major world event that occurred during your president's term in office, such as *The Cuban Missile Crisis*. Then press the <**Enter**> key or <**Tab**> key on your keyboard to move to the next field.

- In the **Major World Events 2** field, explain a second major world event that occurred during your president's term in office, such as *The Soviets built the Berlin Wall*. Then press the <**Enter**> key or <**Tab**> key on your keyboard to move to the next field.

- In the **Other Notes 1** field, type another interesting fact about your president or his term in office, such as *He was one of the youngest presidents who ever lived and the youngest president to die*. Then press the <**Enter**> key or <**Tab**> key on your keyboard to move to the next field.

- In the **Other Notes 2** field, type another interesting fact about your president or his term in office, such as *Kennedy is known for his famous saying, "Ask not what your country can do for you. Ask what you can do for your country."* Then press the <**Enter**> key or <**Tab**> key on your keyboard to move to the next field.

- In the **Picture** field, insert a picture of your president. Here's how:
  - Click in the picture box to select it.

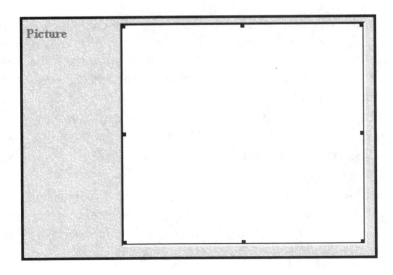

- Click **Insert** on the **Menu** bar.
- Click **Object**.
- At the **Insert Object** dialog box, you have two options—clicking **Create New** or clicking **Create from File**. If you are going to insert a picture from the *Microsoft Clip Gallery*, click **Create New**.

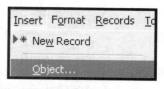

- Click **Microsoft Clip Gallery** under **Object Type**.
- Then click **OK**.
- At the **Microsoft Clip Gallery** dialog box, navigate to the president picture you want.
- Click the president picture to select it.
- Then click the **Insert clip** button.
- Click **OK**.

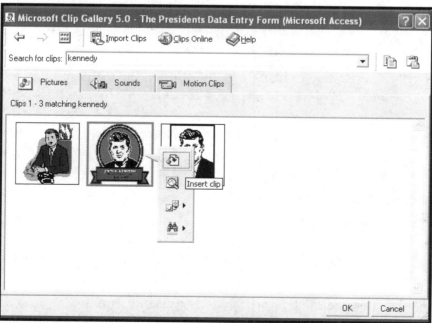

- The president picture now appears in the Picture field.

Major Legislation 2	Kennedy introduced the New Frontier legislation that would stimulate the nation.		Picture	
Major Accomplishments 1	He formed the Alliance for Progress and the Peace Corp.			
Major Accomplishments 2	Kennedy wrote a Pulitzer Prize winning book entitled Profiles in Courage.			
Major World Events 1	The Cuban Missile Crisis			
Major World Events 2	The Soviets built the Berlin Wall			
Other Notes 1	He was the youngest president that ever lived and the youngest president to die.			
Other Notes 2	Kennedy is known for his famous saying, "Ask not what your country can do for you. Ask what you can do for your country."			

Special Note: Several pictures of all the presidents are available in the *Microsoft Design Gallery Live* on the Internet. So, if you search for a president's picture and don't find one in the *Microsoft Clip Gallery*, click the **Clips Online** button. As long as your Web browser is active, you will be taken to the *Microsoft Design Gallery Live* Internet site. There you can download pictures of presidents into the *Microsoft Clip Gallery* on your computer.

- If you are going to insert a picture from a file that you saved in the Presidents Project folder, click **Create from File** in the **Insert Object** dialog box.
- Click the **Browse** button to navigate to the president picture file.
- At the **Browse** dialog box, click the **Look in** list arrow and navigate to the **Presidents Project** folder.
- Click the president picture file you want to select it.
- Click **OK**.
- When you return to the **Insert Object** dialog box, you will see the name of and path to your president picture file in the **File** textbox.
- Click **OK**.
- The president picture now appears in the Picture field.

- Demonstrate to students how to save the information entered into *The Presidents* database by clicking the **Save** button on the **Forms** toolbar.

- Explain and demonstrate to your students how to use the database navigation buttons in the lower left-hand corner of the screen.

  Special Note: Maximize the Presidents Data Entry Form, if necessary, to view the navigation buttons.

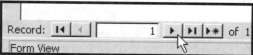

- Also note that if each student will be working in his or her own database, then there won't be many records to navigate. However, it is still important for them to learn how to use the navigation buttons.

- Explain and demonstrate to your students how to print a single record in a database.

  - Click **File** on the **Menu** bar.
  - Click **Print**.
  - At the **Print** dialog box, click **Pages From** under **Print Range**.
  - Type the number of the record from the database that you want to print in both the **From** and **To** boxes, such as *1* and *1*.
  - Click **OK**.

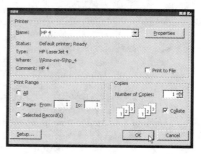

    Special Note: Students **should not** use the **Print** button on the **Forms** toolbar. A Print dialog box **will not** appear after clicking this button. The students will not have the opportunity to designate the record(s) they want printed. **All** the records in the database print when clicking the Print button. This may not be an issue if each student is creating his or her own database, but if the students are all working in one database, a lot of unnecessary printing will occur if they click the Print button.

Producing the Project

Assign each student (or have each student select) a president to research. You will find a list of presidents to research on this page. The ***Presidents to Research*** resource file is also available on the CD-ROM [filename: **pres3.doc**].

Presidents to Research

- George Washington (1789-97)
- John Adams (1797-1801)
- Thomas Jefferson (1801-09)
- James Madison (1809-17)
- James Monroe (1817-25)
- John Quincy Adams (1825-29)
- Andrew Jackson (1829-37)
- Martin Van Buren (1837-41)
- William Henry Harrison (1841)
- John Tyler (1841-45)
- James Polk (1845-49)
- Zachary Taylor (1849-50)
- Millard Fillmore (1850-53)
- Franklin Pierce (1853-57)
- James Buchanan (1857-61)
- Abraham Lincoln (1861-65)
- Andrew Johnson (1865-69)
- Ulysses S. Grant (1869-77)
- Rutherford B. Hayes (1877-81)
- James A. Garfield (1881)
- Chester A. Arthur (1881-85)
- Grover Cleveland (1885-89)
- Benjamin Harrison (1889-93)
- Grover Cleveland (1893-97)
- William McKinley (1897-1901)
- Theodore Roosevelt (1901-09)
- William H. Taft (1909-13)
- Woodrow Wilson (1913-21)
- Warren Harding (1921-23)
- Calvin Coolidge (1923-29)
- Herbert Hoover (1929-33)
- Franklin D. Roosevelt (1933-45)
- Harry S Truman (1945-53)
- Dwight D. Eisenhower (1953-61)
- John F. Kennedy (1961-63)
- Lyndon B. Johnson (1963-69)
- Richard M. Nixon (1969-74)
- Gerald R. Ford (1974-77)
- Jimmy Carter (1977-81)
- Ronald W. Reagan (1981-89)
- George Bush (1989-93)
- William J. Clinton (1993-2001)
- George W. Bush (2001-present)

How to
Make a
Presidential
Portrait

- Take your favorite cereal box.
- Make sure it is empty.

- Cover all six sides of your cereal box with colored paper.

- On the front cover of your cereal box include a picture of your president.
- Then include information about your president, such as his name, political party, years in office, and vice president.

- Create a word game based upon terms related to events that occurred during your president's term in office.
- Place it on the back cover of your cereal box.

- On each side of your box, list at least five interesting details about your president, such as where he was born, where he went to school, his military service, his public service, and more.

Once students complete their research, provide them with the opportunity to enter their findings into *The Presidents* database. Be sure students understand how to find the database on the computer system, open the database, navigate the database, enter their information, save their work, and close the database.

Open the ***How to Make a Presidential Portrait*** presentation file that is partially shown on the previous page [filename: **pres2.ppt**]. Show the presentation to students so they know how to make Presidential Portraits out of cereal boxes. Then provide students with the opportunity to create their Presidential Portraits.

Hand out copies of the ***Presidential Portrait Checklist and Score Sheet*** that is shown on the last page of this project [filename: **pres4.doc**]. Explain to students how to use the checklist to keep organized and aware of the grade they will receive upon completion of their Presidential Portraits.

Presenting the Project

Congratulations! Your students collected presidential information and entered it into a *Microsoft Access* database. They used this information as a foundation for creating Presidential Portraits. You can share *The Presidents* database and the Presidential Portraits in a number of ways:

- Publish *The Presidents* database on your classroom Web site. Then your students' family members and friends across the country (and the world) can view their work. Other students who are learning about the presidents can also use this database as a resource.
- Each day, have a number of students present their Presidential Portraits to the class. Presenters can explain the information displayed on each side of their cereal boxes.
- Display the Presidential Portraits in your classroom and share them with:
  - other classes in your school,
  - your students' parents at an Open House night, or
  - teachers, parents, and others at the next PTSA meeting.

Additional Project Ideas

Now that students have a wealth of information about the presidents at their fingertips, here are some other project ideas:

- Have each student create a timeline related to his or her president's life.
- Have each student create two or three *Microsoft PowerPoint* slides about his or her president. Combine the slides into a multimedia presentation entitled, *The Presidents*.

Additional Resources

The following Internet sites and books will provide you with additional information and educational materials related to the presidents:

Internet Sites

- Visit the PBS **The Presidents** site to learn more about former presidents Reagan, Nixon, Johnson, Kennedy, Eisenhower, Truman, and the Roosevelts. There is even a Teacher's Guide to help you use this Web site in your instruction. The Internet site address is:

    http://www.pbs.org/wgbh/amex/presidents/indexjs.html

- Visit the CSPAN **American Presidents—Life Portraits** site. Pick a president to view his life facts. You can also watch CSPAN programming about each president, visit the portrait gallery, and listen to many of the presidents' speeches. There is also a Teacher Guide, student projects, teaching materials, letters from the presidents, and more. The Internet site address is:

    http://www.americanpresidents.org/

- Visit the White House to view the **Presidents' Hall**. Select any president to learn about his term in office and his life. You can also take a tour of the White House and visit the Kids Only pages to meet Spottie, Barney, and India—the current White House pets—and have some fun. The Internet site address is:

    http://www.whitehouse.gov/history/presidents/index.html

- Visit the Internet Public Library **Presidents of the United States** site. You will find background information, election results, cabinet members, notable events, and some interesting facts about each president. The Internet site address is:

  http://www.ipl.org/ref/POTUS/

- View beautiful **Portraits of the Presidents** from the National Portrait Gallery. You can also read essays and access educational resources. The Internet site address is:

  http://www.npg.si.edu/exh/travpres/index6.htm

- If you want to download some presidential screensavers, you'll love **The American Experience** site. The Internet site address is:

  http://www.pbs.org/wgbh/amex/presidents/frames/screen/screen.html

- Visit the Grolier's **The American Presidency** site. You will find presidential links to campaign sites, presidential libraries, presidential quizzes, and more. The Internet site address is:

  http://gi.grolier.com/presidents/preshome.html

- Visit the USA History **United States Presidents** site. Learn about the presidents and vice presidents. The Internet site address is:

  http://members.tripod.com/~earthdude1/washington/washington.html

Books

- *Look-It-Up Book of Presidents* by Wyatt Blassingame was published in 2001 by Random House [ISBN 0394968395].
- *The Presidents of the United States* by Simon Adams was published in 2001 by Two-Can Publishing [ISBN 1587280930].
- *The Complete Book of Presidents* by American Education Publishing was published in 2001 [ISBN 1561895474].

- *Stuck on the Presidents* by Lara Bergen was published in 2001 by Grosset and Dunlap [ISBN 0448412845].
- *Lives of the Presidents* by Kathleen Krull was published in 1998 by Raintree Steck Vaughn [ISBN 0817240497].
- *Encyclopedia of Presidents and First Ladies* by Children's Press was published in 2000 [ISBN 0516222252].
- *United States Presidents* by Karen Judson, Michael Schuman, and Wendie Cold was published in 1997 by Enslow Publishers [ISBN 0894909126].

Presidential Portrait Checklist and Score Sheet

Name _____ Date _____

President _____

Directions: As you create your presidential portrait, check off your accomplishments. When you are finished, hand this checklist and presidential portrait cereal box project into your teacher for grading.

Check When Done	What to Do	Possible Points	My Score
	I covered a cereal box with paper.	10	
	On the cover, there is a picture of my president and his name.	5	
	On the cover, there is information about my president's political party, the dates he held office, and his vice president.	10	
	On the back, there is a word game. The word game includes at least ten words associated with my president's term in office.	25	
	On one side, there are at least five interesting facts about my president, such as when and where he was born, his early life, his education, his military career (if any), and his political career.	15	
	On the other side, there are at least five interesting facts about my president, such as his family life, his public service, major events during his term in office, and more.	15	
	On the bottom, there is my name.	5	
	My work is free of grammar, punctuation, and spelling errors.	15	
Total		100	

Guess the Great Invention

Project Description

Unlike discoveries, inventions are new human creations that didn't exist before. Inventions are fun and fascinating to students. In this project, students complete two activities:

Students gather data about inventions and record the information in a *Microsoft Access* database.

Then students use this information to create a multimedia presentation entitled, *Guess Which Invention I Am.*

Hardware and Software Needed

The following are the hardware and software applications you will need to complete the two project activities:

Gathering Invention Data

For the first activity in this project, you will need your computer system and *Microsoft Access*. If you choose to have your students complete their research for inventions on the Web, you will also need access to the Internet.

Creating an Inventions Multimedia Presentation

For the second activity in this project, you will need your computer system and a presentation software application, such as *Microsoft PowerPoint*. You will also need access to clip art or digital photographs of inventions. These may be obtained from reference CDs in your classroom, from Web sites, or from the *Microsoft Clip Gallery* within the *Microsoft PowerPoint* program.

Special Note: If you have the resources, make available additional computers on which students can work.

CD-ROM Files

The following files are provided to help you and your students complete this project. All the files are available on the CD-ROM found in the back of this book.

Name of File	Description	Software Application	Filename on the CD-ROM
Inventions	database file	*Microsoft Access*	invent.mdb
Inventions Sample	sample database file	*Microsoft Access*	inventsa.mdb
Guess Which Invention I Am Sample	sample presentation file	*Microsoft PowerPoint*	invensam.ppt
Guess Which Invention I Am Template	presentation template file	*Microsoft PowerPoint*	inventem.ppt
Inventions to Research	resource file	*Microsoft Word*	invenres.doc

Materials Needed and File Preparation

The following are the materials you will need to obtain and the files you will
need to prepare to complete the two project activities:

Gathering Invention Data

- For this activity, provide students with a variety of books about inventions.
  You will find a list of books related to inventions in the **Additional
  Resources** section of this project.

- You may also wish to bookmark several Web sites related to inventions on
  the computer in your classroom. You will find a list of Internet sites related
  to inventions in the **Additional Resources** section of this project.

- Create an **Inventions Project** folder on the hard disk drive of each
  computer that will be used to complete this project. By creating this folder
  on each computer you and your students will have a place to save all the
  files related to this project.

  Special Note: If the computers that students will be using are connected
  via a network, locate the shared network drive and create an Inventions
  Project folder there. Once you place all the files needed for this project in
  this folder, students will be able to access the files from any computer
  connected to the network. Make sure however, that once students open a
  file, they save the file on the hard disk drive of their assigned computer or
  on a floppy disk.

- Send the *Inventions* database file [filename: **invent.mdb**] that is found on
  the CD-ROM to the Inventions Project folder on every computer that will
  be used for this project. Be sure to also turn off the Read-only feature on
  this file on every computer. Alternatively, if the computers are networked,
  simply send the *Inventions* database file to the *Inventions Project* folder you
  set up on the shared drive, and turn off the Read-only feature on the file. (If
  you are not sure how to send the database file to a folder or how to turn off
  the Read-only feature, see the instructions in the Introduction section.)

Creating an Inventions Multimedia Presentation

- For this activity, open each of the following presentation files from the CD-ROM. Save each file to the Inventions Project folder on each computer or save each file to the network.

  - *Guess Which Invention I Am Sample* [filename: **invensam.ppt**]
  - *Guess Which Invention I Am Template* [filename: **inventem.ppt**].

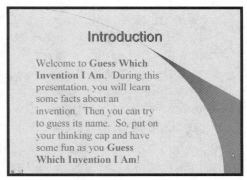

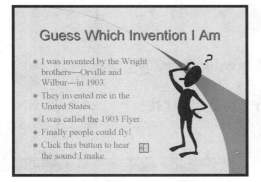

Introducing the Project

Open and display the *Guess Which Invention I Am Sample* presentation file that is partially shown on the previous page [filename: **invensam.ppt**]. Encourage students to interact with the presentation. Allow students to guess the inventions that are displayed.

Explain to students that they will complete a two-part project about inventions:

- First, students will collect data about inventions and enter the information they find in a *Microsoft Access* database. The information they will need includes the names of the inventions, the names of the inventors, when the inventions were created, where the inventions were created, why the inventions were important, and any other information they would like to include about inventions. Students may also enter pictures, sounds, and movie clips related to their inventions.

- Second, students will use the information they gathered to create a multimedia presentation of their inventions entitled, *Guess Which Invention I Am*, to share with others.

First show the students an example of a completed *Inventions* database:

- Launch *Microsoft Access*.

- Open the *Inventions Sample* database file from the CD-ROM [filename: **inventsa.mdb**].

  Special Note: A dialog box will appear informing you that the database is Read-only. This is fine since you will only be viewing, not changing, this sample database. Click **OK**.

- At the **inventsa** database dialog box, click **Forms** under the **Objects Bar**.

- Click **Invention Information** under the **Objects List**.

- Click **Open**.

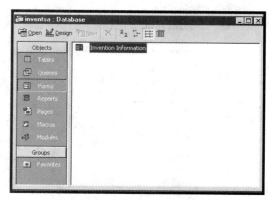

- The *Invention Information* table, displayed in **Form View**, will appear on your screen.

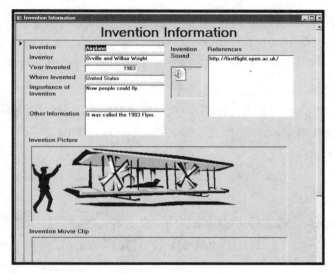

- Explain to students that this is a sample *Invention Information* form. They will be creating one just like it with information that they gather about a particular invention.
- Explain and demonstrate the features of *Invention Information* form as follows:
    - Explain to students that the black labels are the names of fields in database. Elicit from students the names of the fields they see, such as Invention, Inventor, Year Invented, Where Invented, Importance of Invention, and more.
    - Explain to students that the white text boxes next to the labels are where they will enter information about an invention. The gray boxes are where they enter sounds, pictures, and movie clips related to their inventions.
- Take a moment to view some of the example data on the invention of the airplane.

    Special Note: A movie clip of an airplane was not available, so the field was left empty. However, there are many movie clips of inventions in the *Microsoft Clip Gallery* for your students to insert.

- Close the ***Inventions Sample*** database file.

Now open and demonstrate to students how to use the *Inventions* database file template. Here's how:

- Open the ***Inventions*** database file from your *Inventions Project* folder [filename: **invent.mdb**].

  Special Note: Prior to opening the file, be sure that the Read-only feature is turned off.

- At the **Invent** database dialog box, click **Forms** under the **Objects Bar**.
- Click **Invention Information** under the **Objects List**.
- Click **Open**.
- An empty Inventions table, displayed in **Form View,** will appear on your screen.

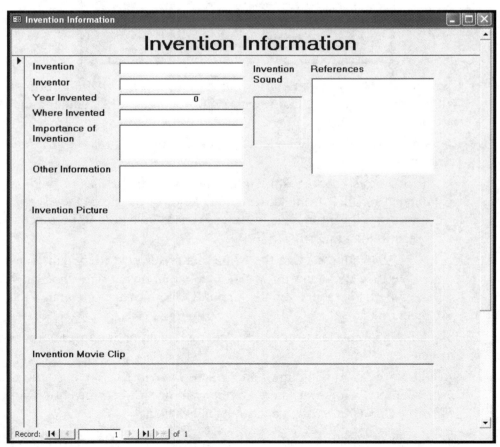

Using the data provided in the instructions below, explain and demonstrate how students should enter data into each field as follows:

- Click in the **Invention** field and type the name of your invention, such as the *airplane*. Then press the **<Enter>** key or **<Tab>** key on your keyboard to move to the next field.

- In the **Inventor** field, type the name(s) of the creator(s) of the invention, such as *Orville and Wilbur Wright*. Then press the **<Enter>** key or **<Tab>** key on your keyboard to move to the next field.

- In the **Year Invented** field, type the year the invention was created, such as *1903*. Then press the **<Enter>** key or **<Tab>** key on your keyboard to move to the next field.

- In the **Where Invented** field, type the country in which the invention was created, such as the *United States*. Then press the **<Enter>** key or **<Tab>** key on your keyboard to move to the next field.

- In the **Importance of Invention** file, type at least one reason why the invention was important, such as *Now people could fly.* Then press the **<Enter>** key or **<Tab>** key on your keyboard to move to the next field.

- In the **Other Information** field, type another fact about the invention, such as *It was called the 1903 Flyer.* Then press the **<Enter>** key or **<Tab>** key on your keyboard to move to the next field.

- In the **Invention Sound** field, insert a sound file that represents your invention, if possible. Here's how:

  - Click in the **Invention Sound** box to select it.

  - Click **Insert** on the **Menu** bar.

  - Click **Object**.

- At the **Insert Object** dialog box, click **Create from File**.

- Then click the **Browse** button.

- Navigate to the folder where your sound file is located (see **Special Note** on the following page to locate sound files).

- Click the file to select it.

- Click **OK**.

- When you return to the **Insert Object** dialog box, you will see the path to your sound file listed in the **File** text box. Click **OK**.

- When you return to your database, you will see a sound icon. Double-click the icon to test your invention sound.

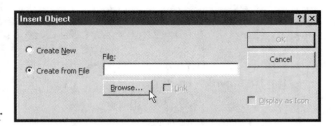

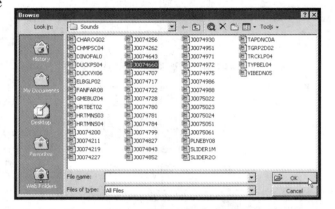

Special Note: The best place to find sound files is in the *Microsoft Clip Gallery*. However, *Microsoft Access* does not allow you to insert sound files directly from the *Microsoft Clip Gallery*. So, you will need to locate a sound file that you like in the *Microsoft Clip Gallery* and then find where it is residing on your computer system. Then you can navigate to it and select it for insertion into your database.

The easiest way to do this is to find the sound file in the ***Microsoft Clip Gallery*** and right-click it (to open the *Microsoft Clip Gallery* in *Microsoft Access*, right-click the Invention Sound box and choose **Insert Object.** Click **Create New** and choose *Microsoft Clip Gallery* from the Object Type list, then click **OK**. Click the Sounds tab to locate a sound file). When you do, a pop-up menu appears. Select **Clip Properties**. At the **Clip Properties** window on the **Description** tab under **File Information**, you will see the filename of your sound clip and the path information that indicates where it is residing on your computer system. Write down these pieces of information so you can use them when you browse to your sound file, then close the *Microsoft Clip Gallery* window. You have just learned how to bypass the *Microsoft Clip Gallery* and insert the sound file you want in your database.

- In the **References** field, enter the sources of your information about the invention, such as ***http://firstflight.open.ac.uk/***. You can copy and paste Web site addresses into this field as well as type the titles and authors of books and other reference material. Press the **<Enter>** key or **<Tab>** key on your keyboard to move to the next field.

- In the **Invention Picture** field, insert a picture file that represents your invention, if one is available. Here's how:

    - Click in the **Invention Picture** box to select it.

    - Click **Insert** on the **Menu** bar.

    - Click **Object**.

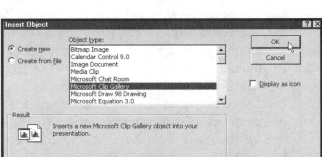

    - At the **Insert Object** dialog box, you have two options—clicking **Create New** or clicking **Create from File**. If you are going to insert a picture from the *Microsoft Clip Gallery*, click **Create New**.

    - Click **Microsoft Clip Gallery** under **Object Type**.

    - Then click **OK**.

    - At the **Microsoft Clip Gallery** dialog box, navigate to the invention picture you want.

    - Click on the invention picture to select it.

    - Then click the **Insert clip** button.

- The invention picture now appears in the Invention Picture field.

- If you are going to insert a picture from a file that you saved in the Inventions Project folder, click **Create from File** at the **Insert Object** dialog box.

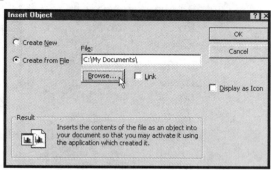

- Click the **Browse** button to navigate to the invention picture file.

- At the **Browse** dialog box, click the **Look in** list arrow and navigate to the Inventions Project folder.

- Click the invention picture file you want to select it.

- Click **OK**.

- When you return to the **Insert Object** dialog box, you will see the name of and path to your invention picture file in the **File** textbox.

- Click **OK**.

- When you return to your database, the invention picture appears in the Picture field.

- In the **Invention Movie Clip** field, insert a movie clip of your invention, if one is available. Follow the instructions previously provided for inserting a picture from the *Microsoft Clip Gallery*. Just be sure to select the **Motion Clips** tab when you are in the *Microsoft Clip Gallery*.

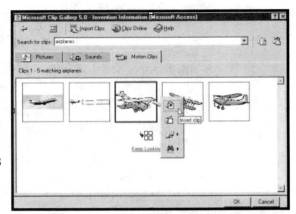

- If you are inserting a movie clip from a file, follow the instructions previously provided for inserting a picture from a file.

- Demonstrate to students how to save the information entered into the *Inventions* database by clicking the **Save** button on the **Forms** toolbar.

- Explain and demonstrate to your students how to use the database navigation buttons in the lower left-hand corner of the screen.

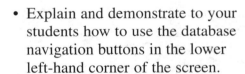

Special Note: Maximize the Invention Information form if necessary to view the navigation buttons.

Also note that if each student will be working in his or her own database, then there won't be many records to navigate. However, it is still important for them to learn how to use the navigation buttons.

- Explain and demonstrate to your students how to print a single record in a database. Here's how:

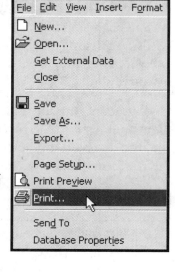

  - Click **File** on the **Menu** bar.

  - Click **Print**.

  - At the **Print** dialog box, click **Pages From** under **Print Range**.

  - Type the number of the record from the database that you want to print in both the **From** and **To** boxes, such as *1* and *1*.

  - Click **OK**.

    Special Note: Students **should not** use the **Print** button on the **Forms** toolbar. A Print dialog box **will not** appear after clicking this button. The students will not have the opportunity to designate the record(s) they want printed. **All** the records in the database print when

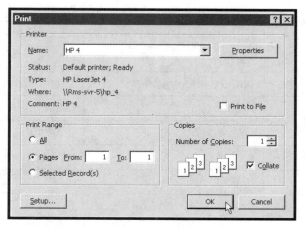

clicking the Print button. This may not be an issue if each student is creating his or her own database, but if the students are all working in one database, a lot of unnecessary printing will occur if they click the Print button.

Producing the Project

Assign each student (or have each student select) an invention to research. You will find a list of more than 60 inventions to research on the following page. The *Inventions to Research* resource file is also available on the CD-ROM [filename: **invenres.doc**].

Once students complete their research, provide them with the opportunity to enter their findings into the *Inventions* database. Be sure students understand how to find the database on the computer, open the database, navigate the database, enter their information, save their work, and close the database.

Inventions to Research

1.	airplane	21.	garbage disposal	41.	printing press
2.	airship (dirigible)	22.	gyroscope	42.	radar
3.	automobile	23.	harvester (thresher)	43.	radio
4.	balloon (aviation)	24.	helicopter	44.	railroad sleeping car
5.	barometer	25.	jet propulsion	45.	rayon
6.	battery (electric)	26.	lawn mower	46.	refrigerator
7.	burner (gas)	27.	lightning rod	47.	rocket engine
8.	camera (Kodak)	28.	linoleum	48.	rubber
9.	cash register	29.	locomotive	49.	satellite
10.	cellophane	30.	loom (power)	50.	sewing machine
11.	cement	31.	match (friction)	51.	steam engine
12.	cotton gin	32.	microscope	52.	steel
13.	dental plate (rubber)	33.	motorcycle	53.	stethoscope
14.	diesel engine	34.	movies (silent)	54.	submarine
15.	dynamite	35.	movies (sound)	55.	telegraph
16.	electromagnet	36.	nuclear reactor	56.	telephone
17.	evaporated milk	37.	nylon	57.	telescope
18.	elevator	38.	oleomargarine	58.	toaster

Inventions to Research					
19.	flying shuttle	39.	phonograph	59.	typewriter
20.	fountain pen	40.	piano	60.	vacuum cleaner

Open the ***Guess Which Invention I Am Template*** presentation file [filename: **inventem.ppt**]. Add your name as the teacher to the Title slide.

Then skip or make changes to the Introduction slide. It's up to you!

Explain to students that they will each be completing two slides—one that provides the "guessing" information about the invention and one that displays the name and picture of the invention. Demonstrate to students how to complete their first slides as follows, using the sample information provided:

- On the first "guessing" slide, click after the text *I was invented by* and enter the name or names of the inventor(s) and the invention date, such as ***Elias Howe, Jr. in 1846***.
- Press the **<Enter>** key on your keyboard to move to the next line.

- At the second bullet, type a sentence that indicates where the invention was created, such as ***He invented me in the United States***.
- Press the **\<Enter>** key on your keyboard to move to the next line.
- At the third bullet, type a sentence that explains why the invention was important, such as ***I could work as rapidly as nine tailors***.
- Press the **\<Enter>** key on your keyboard to move to the next line.
- At the fourth bullet, type a sentence that tells some other interesting fact about your invention.

    —or—

- If you were able to locate a sound file for your invention, try this: at the fourth bullet, type instructions for listening to the sound of the invention, such as ***Click this button to hear the sound I make***.

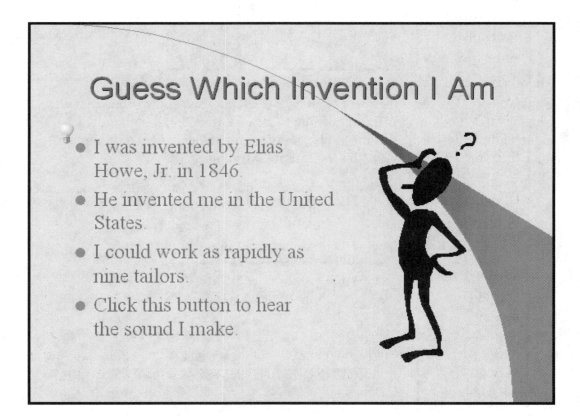

Guess Which Invention I Am

- I was invented by Elias Howe, Jr. in 1846.
- He invented me in the United States.
- I could work as rapidly as nine tailors.
- Click this button to hear the sound I make.

- Click elsewhere on the screen to deselect the text box area and to view the information you just entered.

- To add a sound to your invention slide, complete the following:

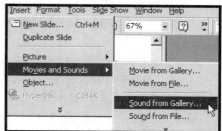

- Click **Insert** on the **Menu** bar.

- Click **Movies and Sounds**.

- If your sound file is in the *Microsoft Clip Gallery*, click **Sound from Gallery**.

- At the **Insert Sound** dialog box, click in the **Search for clips** text box and type the name of your invention, such as *sewing machine*.

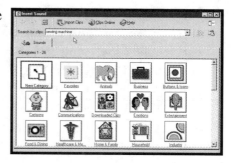

- Press the **<Enter>** key on your keyboard to activate the search.

- When the sound files appear, click the sound file you want.

- Then click **Insert clip**.

    Special Note: If you don't see the sound file you want, search the *Microsoft Clip Gallery* on the Internet. Click the **Clips online** button. Then search for, select, and download the sound file.

- Click the **Close** button on the title bar of the **Insert Sound** dialog box to return to your slide.

- A *Microsoft PowerPoint* dialog box appears, asking if you want the sound to automatically play when the slide appears in your presentation. Choose **No** to have the sound play when you click it.

- The sound icon will appear in the middle of your screen. Click and drag it to the location you want, such as right after the sentence *Click this button to hear the sound I make*.

- Click elsewhere on the screen to deselect the sound icon.
- Test the sound icon by double-clicking it.

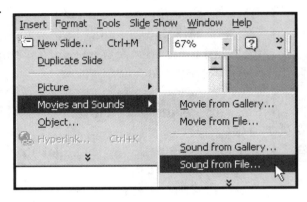

- If your students are adding sound clips from sound files, the instructions are a little bit different—up to the point of clicking **No** at the *Microsoft PowerPoint* dialog box.
- Click **Insert** on the **Menu** bar.
- Click **Movies and Sounds**.
- Click **Sound from File**.
- At the **Insert Sound** dialog box, click the **Look in** list arrow and navigate to the folder where the sound file is saved.
- Click the sound file to select it.
- Click **OK**.

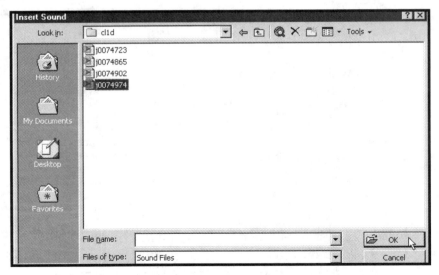

Demonstrate to students how to complete their second slides as follows:

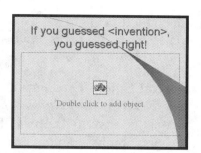

- Remove the **<invention>** name placeholder and type the name of your invention.

- If you are adding a picture from the *Microsoft Clip Gallery*, double-click in the **Double click to add object** area.

- At the **Insert Object** dialog box, click *Microsoft Clip Gallery* under **Object type**.

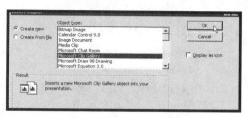

- Then click **OK**.

- At the *Microsoft Clip Gallery* dialog box, navigate to the picture you want, such as a sewing machine.

- Click the picture to select it.

- Then click **Insert clip**.

- That's it! The picture will automatically appear on your slide.

- If you are adding a picture from a file, double-click in the **Double click to add object** area.

- At the **Insert Object** dialog box, click **Create from file**.

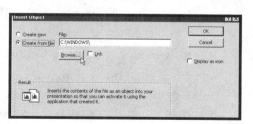

- Then click the **Browse** button.

- Navigate to the folder where you saved your picture file.

- Click the picture file to select it.

- Then click **OK**.

- When you return to the **Insert Object** dialog box, click **OK**.

- That's it! The picture will automatically appear on your slide.

One at a time, help students complete their slides. Then help students proofread the slides carefully and make any necessary corrections before sharing their *Guess Which Invention I Am* presentations with others.

Special Note: If students are working at multiple computers, have each student work on their own ***Guess Which Invention I Am Template*** presentation file [filename: **inventem.ppt**]. Then, assemble all of the students' slides into one presentation by copying and pasting slides into one file.

Presenting the Project

Congratulations! Your students collected invention information and entered it into a *Microsoft Access* database. They used this information as a foundation for creating a multimedia presentation about inventions. You can share the *Guess Which Invention I Am* multimedia presentation in a number of ways:

- Print the *Guess Which Invention I Am* multimedia presentation and create an inventions bulletin board. Place the title slide at the top or in the center of your bulletin board. Then place each printed invention information slide over its related invention answer slide. Using staples or push pins, tack each set of slide printouts to the bulletin board. Secure the top two corners only. That way, students can read about an invention and lift the top printed slide to view the answer on the bottom slide.

- Present *Guess Which Invention I Am* to:
  - other classes in your school,
  - your students' parents at an Open House night, or
  - teachers, parents, and others at the next PTSA meeting.

- Publish the *Guess Which Invention I Am* multimedia presentation on your classroom Web site. Then your students' family members and friends across the country (and the world) can view their work.

- Print the *Guess Which Invention I Am* multimedia presentation and bind it for your classroom library.

- Publish the *Inventions* database file on your classroom Web site. Then other students who are learning about and researching inventions will have a wonderful source of information.

Additional Project Ideas

Now that students have a wealth of information about inventions at their fingertips, have them create an inventions timeline.

Additional Resources

The following Internet sites and books will provide you with additional information and educational materials related to inventions:

Internet Sites

- Visit the National Geographic World Inventions site. You can play an invention game, view lists of invention books and Internet sites, and even create your own invention. The Internet site address is:

    http://www.nationalgeographic.com/features/96/inventions/index.html

- Visit this ThinkQuest site to learn about 12 of the greatest inventors who ever lived. The Internet site address is:

    http://www.thinkquest.org/library/lib/site_sum_outside.html?tname=5847&cid=2&url=5847

- Visit this Kids' Club site to view an invention timeline. The Internet site address is:

    http://www.cbc4kids.ca/general/the-lab/history-of-invention/default.html

- Visit this Yahooligan's index to view a list of Internet sites related to 68 inventors. This is a great place to start your research! The Internet site address is:

    http://www.yahooligans.com/science_and_nature/machines/inventions/Inventors/

- Visit the National Inventors Hall of Fame site and follow the links to invention sites, invention competitions, and other pages for kids. The Internet site address is:

    http://www.invent.org/

- Visit the Inventors Museum and search their database of inventors, including African American inventors and women inventors. The Internet site address is:

    http://www.inventorsmuseum.com/museum_map.htm

Books

- *Inventions That Shaped World History* by Bill Yenne was published in 1993 by Bluewood Books [ISBN 0912517026].

- *Inventors and Inventions* by Lorraine Hopping Eagin was published in 1999 by Scholastic Trade [ISBN 0590103881].

- *Toilets, Toasters, and Telephones* by Susan Goldman Rubin was published in 1998 by Browndeer Press [ISBN 0152014217].

- *Eyewitness—Inventions* by Lionel Bender was published in 2000 by DK Publishing [ISBN 0789465760].

- *Great Inventors and Inventions* by Bruce Lafontaine was publishing in 1998 by Dover Publishing [ISBN 0486297845].

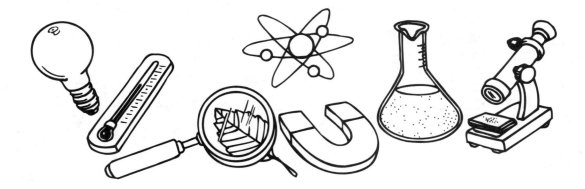

Fruit Pie

Did you know that although dietary guidelines recommend that children eat at least five servings of fruits and vegetables each day, a recent USDA study revealed that nearly half of all elementary school age children eat no fruit on any given day? So, helping students learn more about fruit is one way to encourage more healthful eating habits.

Project Description

In this project students learn about the nutritional values of a variety of fruits, while completing two activities:

1. First, students gather data about fruits and record the information in a *Microsoft Access* database.

2. Second, each student creates a "fruit pie" using the information gathered about the fruit and a variety of art supplies.

Hardware and Software Needed

The following are the hardware and software applications you will need to complete the two project activities:

Gathering Fruit Data

For the first activity in this project, you will need your computer system and *Microsoft Access*. If you choose to have your students complete their research of fruit on the Web, you will also need access to the Internet.

Creating a "Fruit Pie"

For the second activity in this project, you will need your computer system and a word processing software application, such as *Microsoft Word*. This will enable your students to create components of the "fruit pie" on the computer.

CD-ROM Files

The following files are provided to help you and your students complete this project. All the files are available on the CD-ROM found in the back of this book.

Name of File	Description	Software Application	Filename on the CD-ROM
Fruit Pie	database file	*Microsoft Access*	fruit1.mdb
Fruit Pie Sample	sample database file	*Microsoft Access*	fruitsa.mdb
How to Make a "Fruit Pie"	presentation file	*Microsoft PowerPoint*	fruit2.doc
Fruits to Research	resource file	*Microsoft Word*	fruit3.doc
"Fruit Pie" Checklist and Score Sheet	organizer and score sheet	*Microsoft Word*	fruit4.doc

Materials Needed and File Preparation

The following are the materials you will need to obtain and the files you will need to prepare to complete the two project activities:

Gathering Fruit Data

- For this activity, provide students with a variety of books about fruit. You will find a list of books related to fruit in the **Additional Resources** section of this project.
- You may also wish to bookmark several Web sites related to fruit on the computer in your classroom. You will find a list of Internet sites related to fruit in the **Additional Resources** section of this project.

194

- Create a **Fruit Pie Project** folder on the hard disk drive of each computer that will be used to complete this project. By creating this folder on each computer you and your students will have a place to save all the files related to this project.

  Special Note: If the computers that students will be using are connected via a network, locate the shared network drive and create a Fruit Pie Project folder there. Once you place all the files needed for this project in this folder, students will be able to access the files from any computer connected to the network. Make sure however, that once students open a file, they save the file on the hard disk drive of their assigned computer or on a floppy disk.

- Send the ***Fruit Pie*** database file [filename: **fruit1.mdb**] that is found on the CD-ROM to the Fruit Pie Project folder on every computer that will be used for this project. Be sure to also turn off the Read-only feature on this file on every computer. Alternatively, if the computers are networked, simply send the *Fruit Pie* database file to the Fruit Pie Project folder you set up on the shared drive, and turn off the Read-only feature on the file there. (If you are not sure how to send the database file to a folder or how to turn off the Read-only feature, see the instructions in the Introduction section.)

Creating "Fruit Pie"

- For this activity, open the ***How to Make a "Fruit Pie"*** [filename: **fruit2.ppt**] presentation file from the CD-ROM. Save it to the Fruit Pie Project folder on each computer or save the file to the network.

- Make copies of the ***Fruit Pie Checklist and Score Sheet*** that is displayed on the last page of this project. You can copy this page from the book or open and print the file from the CD-ROM [filename: **fruit 4.doc**].

Introducing the Project

Share with students **The Food Pyramid** that is shown on the following page. Have students identify the food groups and the number of servings they should eat each day. Explain to students that they will be focusing on the Fruit Group as they complete the following two-part project:

- First, students will collect data about a fruit and enter the information they find in a *Microsoft Access* database. The information they will need includes the name of the fruit; the type or variety of the fruit; the serving size; the amount of fat, cholesterol, sodium, and potassium in the fruit; the carbohydrate, sugar, fiber, and protein values of the fruit; the percentage of vitamins and minerals in the fruit; eight fruit facts; and a picture of the fruit.

- Second, each student will use the information he or she gathered to create a "fruit pie."

Demonstrate to students how to find the information they will need for their database from a food label. You will find a sample food label for an avocado on the following page. (You may wish to print copies of this food label to hand out to students, so they can follow along.) Refer to this food label as you enter nutrition information into the *Fruit Pie* database.

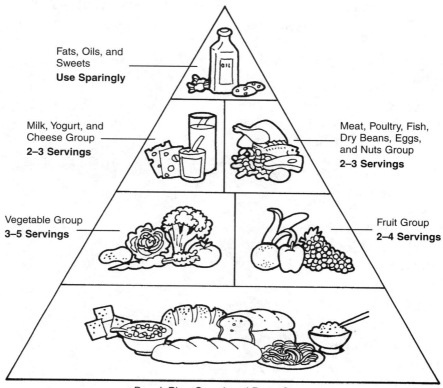

Fats, Oils, and Sweets
Use Sparingly

Milk, Yogurt, and Cheese Group
2–3 Servings

Meat, Poultry, Fish, Dry Beans, Eggs, and Nuts Group
2–3 Servings

Vegetable Group
3–5 Servings

Fruit Group
2–4 Servings

Bread, Rice, Cereal, and Pasta Group
6–11 Servings

Avocado Nutrition Facts

Nutrition Facts

Serving Size 1/5 medium (30g/1.1 oz)

Amount Per Serving	
Calories 55	Calories from Fat 45

	% Daily Value*
Total Fat 5g	**8%**
Saturated Fat 1g	**5%**
Polyunsaturated Fat 1g	
Monounsaturated Fat 3g	
Cholesterol 0mg	**0%**
Sodium 0mg	**0%**
Potassium 170mg	**5%**
Total Carbohydrate 3g	**1%**
Dietary Fiber 3g	**12%**
Sugars 0g	
Protein 1g	

Vitamin A 0%	•	Vitamin C 4%
Calcium 0%	•	Iron 0%
Vitamin E 4%	•	Riboflavin 2%
Niacin 2%	•	Vitamin B6 4%
Folate 6%	•	Pantothenic Acid 2%
Magnesium 2%		

*Percent Daily Values are based on a 2,000 calorie diet. Your daily values may be higher or lower depending on your calorie needs:

	Calories:	2,000	2,500
Total Fat	Less than	65g	80g
Saturated Fat	Less than	20g	25g
Cholesterol	Less than	300mg	300mg
Sodium	Less than	2,400mg	2,400mg
Potassium		3,500mg	3,500mg
Total Carbohydrate		300g	375g
Dietary Fiber		25g	30g

Now show the students an example of a completed *Fruit Pie* database:

- Launch *Microsoft Access*.

Open the *Fruit Pie Sample* database file from the CD-ROM [filename: **fruitsa.mdb**].

> **Special Note:** A dialog box will appear informing you that the database is Read-only. This is fine since you will only be viewing, not changing, this sample database. Click **OK**.

- At the **fruitsa** database dialog box, click **Forms** under the **Objects Bar**.
- Click **Fruit Data Entry Form** under the **Objects List**.
- Click **Open**.
- The Fruit Pie table, displayed in **Form View**, will appear on your screen.

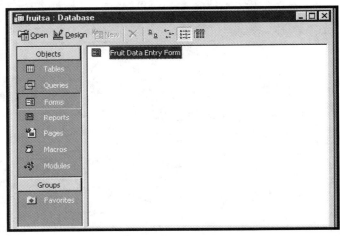

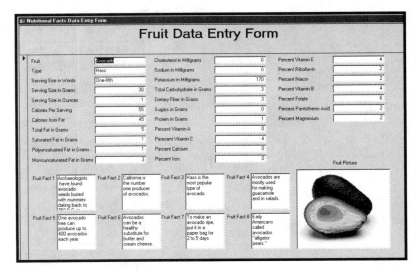

- Explain to students that this is a sample Fruit Data Entry Form. They will be creating one just like it with information that they gather about a particular fruit.
- Explain and demonstrate the features of Fruit Data Entry Form as follows:
  - Point out to students that the black text represents the names of fields in database. Elicit from students the names of the fields they see, such as Fruit, Type, Serving Size in Words, and more.
  - Explain to students that the white text boxes next to the black text are where they will enter information about a fruit.
- Take a moment to view some of the example data on the avocado.
- Close the ***Fruit Pie Sample*** database file.
- Now open and demonstrate to students how to use the *Fruit Pie* database file template. Here's how:
- Open the ***Fruit Pie*** database file from your **Fruit Pie Project** folder [filename: **fruit1.mdb**].

  Special Note: Prior to opening the file, be sure that the Read-only feature is turned off.

- At the **fruit1** database dialog box, click **Forms** under the **Objects Bar**.
- Click **Fruit Data Entry Form** under the **Objects** list.
- Click **Open**.
- An empty Fruit Pie table, displayed in **Form View,** will appear on your screen.

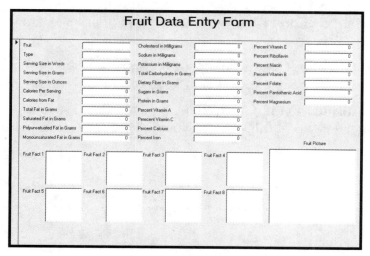

- Using the data provided in the instructions below, explain and demonstrate how students should enter data into each field as follows:

- Click in the **Fruit** field and type the name of your fruit, such as *avocado*. Then press the <Enter> key or <Tab> key on your keyboard to move to the next field.

- In the **Type** field, type the type or variety of the fruit, such as *Hass*. Then press the <Enter> key or <Tab> key on your keyboard to move to the next field.

- In the **Serving Size in Words** field, type the serving size, such as *one-fifth*. Then press the <Enter> key or <Tab> key on your keyboard to move to the next field.

- In the **Serving Size in Grams** field, type the value, such as *30*. Then press the <Enter> key or <Tab> key on your keyboard to move to the next field.

- In the **Serving Size in Ounces** field, type the value, such as *1*. Then press the <Enter> key or <Tab> key on your keyboard to move to the next field.

   Special Note: This field is set up to round to the nearest ounce. So, if you enter a value such as 1.1, the field will display 1 ounce. If you enter a value of 1.7, the field will display 2 ounces.

- In the **Calories Per Serving** field, type the number of calories, such as *55*. Then press the <Enter> key or <Tab> key on your keyboard to move to the next field.

- In the **Calories from Fat** field, type the number of calories, such as *45*. Then press the <Enter> key or <Tab> key on your keyboard to move to the next field.

- In the **Total Fat in Grams** field, type the value, such as *5*. Then press the <Enter> key or <Tab> key on your keyboard to move to the next field.

- In the **Saturated Fat in Grams** field, type the value, such as *1*. Then press the <Enter> key or <Tab> key on your keyboard to move to the next field.

- In the **Polyunsaturated Fat in Grams** field, type the value, such as *1*. Then press the <**Enter**> key or <**Tab**> key on your keyboard to move to the next field.

- In the **Monounsaturated Fat in Grams** field, type the value, such as *3*. Then press the <**Enter**> key or <**Tab**> key on your keyboard to move to the next field.

- In the **Cholesterol in Milligrams** field, type the value, such as *0*. Then press the <**Enter**> key or <**Tab**> key on your keyboard to move to the next field.

- In the **Sodium in Milligrams** field, type the value, such as *0*. Then press the <**Enter**> key or <**Tab**> key on your keyboard to move to the next field.

- In the **Potassium in Milligrams** field, type the value, such as *170*. Then press the <**Enter**> key or <**Tab**> key on your keyboard to move to the next field.

- In the **Total Carbohydrate in Grams** field, type the value, such as *3*. Then press the <**Enter**> key or <**Tab**> key on your keyboard to move to the next field.

- In the **Dietary Fiber in Grams** field, type the value, such as *3*. Then press the <**Enter**> key or <**Tab**> key on your keyboard to move to the next field.

- In the **Sugars in Grams** field, type the value, such as *0*. Then press the <**Enter**> key or <**Tab**> key on your keyboard to move to the next field.

- In the **Protein in Grams** field, type the value, such as *1*. Then press the <**Enter**> key or <**Tab**> key on your keyboard to move to the next field.

- In the **Percent Vitamin A** field, type the percent, such as *0*. Then press the <**Enter**> key or <**Tab**> key on your keyboard to move to the next field.

- In the **Percent Vitamin C** field, type the percent, such as *4*. Then press the <**Enter**> key or <**Tab**> key on your keyboard to move to the next field.

- In the **Percent Calcium** field, type the percent, such as *0*. Then press the <**Enter**> key or <**Tab**> key on your keyboard to move to the next field.

- In the **Percent Iron** field, type the percent, such as *0*. Then press the <**Enter**> key or <**Tab**> key on your keyboard to move to the next field.

- In the **Percent Vitamin E** field, type the percent, such as *4*. Then press the <**Enter**> key or <**Tab**> key on your keyboard to move to the next field.

- In the **Percent Riboflavin** field, type the percent, such as *2*. Then press the <**Enter**> key or <**Tab**> key on your keyboard to move to the next field.

- In the **Percent Niacin** field, type the percent, such as *2*. Then press the <**Enter**> key or <**Tab**> key on your keyboard to move to the next field.

- In the **Percent Vitamin B** field, type the percent, such as *4*. Then press the <**Enter**> key or <**Tab**> key on your keyboard to move to the next field.

- In the **Percent Folate** field, type the percent, such as *6*. Then press the <**Enter**> key or <**Tab**> key on your keyboard to move to the next field.

- In the **Percent Pantothenic Acid** field, type the percent, such as *2*. Then press the <**Enter**> key or <**Tab**> key on your keyboard to move to the next field.

- In the **Percent Magnesium** field, type the percent, such as *2*. Then press the <**Enter**> key or <**Tab**> key on your keyboard to move to the next field.

- In the **Fruit Fact 1** field, type an interesting fact about your fruit, such as *Archaeologists have found avocado seeds buried with mummies dating back to 740 B.C. in Peru.* Then press the <**Enter**> key or <**Tab**> key on your keyboard to move to the next field.

- In the **Fruit Fact 2** field, type a second interesting fact about your fruit, such as *California is the number one producer of avocados.* Then press the <**Enter**> key or <**Tab**> key on your keyboard to move to the next field.

- In the **Fruit Fact 3** field, type a third interesting fact about your fruit, such as *Hass is the most popular type of avocado.* Then press the <**Enter**> key or <**Tab**> key on your keyboard to move to the next field.

- In the **Fruit Fact 4** field, type a fourth interesting fact about your fruit, such as *Avocados are mostly used for making guacamole and in salads.* Then press the <**Enter**> key or <**Tab**> key on your keyboard to move to the next field.

- In the **Fruit Fact 5** field, type a fifth interesting fact about your fruit, such as *One avocado tree can produce up to 400 avocados each year.* Then press the <**Enter**> key or <**Tab**> key on your keyboard to move to the next field.

- In the **Fruit Fact 6** field, type a sixth interesting fact about your fruit, such as *Avocados can be a healthy substitute for butter and cream cheese.* Then press the <**Enter**> key or <**Tab**> key on your keyboard to move to the next field.

- In the **Fruit Fact 7** field, type a seventh interesting fact about your fruit, such as *To make an avocado ripe, put it in a paper bag for 2 to 5 days.* Then press the <**Enter**> key or <**Tab**> key on your keyboard to move to the next field.

- In the **Fruit Fact 8** field, type an eighth interesting fact about your fruit, such as *Early Americans called avocados "alligator pears."* Then press the <**Enter**> key or <**Tab**> key on your keyboard to move to the next field.

- In the **Fruit Picture** field, insert a picture of your fruit, if there is one available. Here's how:

  - Click in the picture box to select it.
  - Click **Insert** on the **Menu** bar.
  - Click **Object**.
  - At the **Insert Object** dialog box, you have two options—clicking **Create New** or clicking **Create from File**. If you are going to insert a picture from the *Microsoft Clip Gallery*, click **Create New**.

  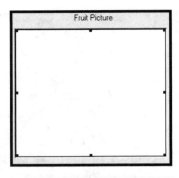

  - Click **Microsoft Clip Gallery** under **Object Type**.
  - Then click **OK**.

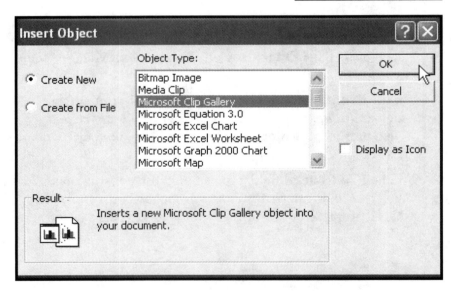

- At the **Microsoft Clip Gallery** dialog box, search for or navigate to the fruit picture you want.
- Click the fruit picture to select it.
- Then click the **Insert clip** button.
- When you return to your database, the fruit picture appears in the Picture field.

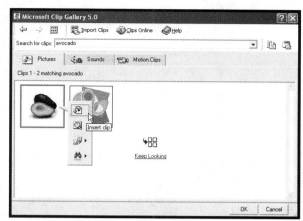

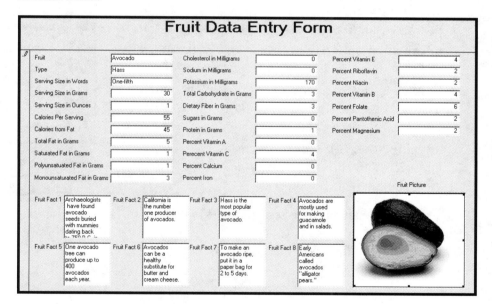

Fruit Data Entry Form

Fruit	Avocado	Cholesterol in Milligrams	0	Percent Vitamin E	4
Type	Hass	Sodium in Milligrams	0	Percent Riboflavin	2
Serving Size in Words	One-fifth	Potassium in Milligrams	170	Percent Niacin	2
Serving Size in Grams	30	Total Carbohydrate in Grams	3	Percent Vitamin B	4
Serving Size in Ounces	1	Dietary Fiber in Grams	3	Percent Folate	6
Calories Per Serving	55	Sugars in Grams	0	Percent Pantothenic Acid	2
Calories from Fat	45	Protein in Grams	1	Percent Magnesium	2
Total Fat in Grams	5	Percent Vitamin A	0		
Saturated Fat in Grams	1	Perecent Vitamin C	4		
Polyunsaturated Fat in Grams	1	Percent Calcium	0		
Monounsaturated Fat in Grams	3	Percent Iron	0		

Fruit Picture

Fruit Fact 1 Archaeologists have found avocado seeds buried with mummies dating back	Fruit Fact 2 California is the number one producer of avocados.	Fruit Fact 3 Hass is the most popular type of avocado.	Fruit Fact 4 Avocados are mostly used for making guacamole and in salads.
Fruit Fact 5 One avocado tree can produce up to 400 avocados each year.	Fruit Fact 6 Avocados can be a healthy substitute for butter and cream cheese.	Fruit Fact 7 To make an avocado ripe, put it in a paper bag for 2 to 5 days.	Fruit Fact 8 Early Americans called avocados "alligator pears."

- If you are going to insert a picture from a file that you saved in the Fruit Pie Project folder, click **Create from File** at the **Insert Object** dialog box.
- Click the **Browse** button to navigate to the fruit picture file.
- At the **Browse** dialog box, click the **Look in** list arrow and navigate to the **Fruit Pie Project** folder.
- Click the fruit picture file you want to select it.
- Click **OK**.
- When you return to the **Insert Object** dialog box, you will see the name of and path to your fruit picture file in the **File** textbox.
- Click **OK**.
- When you return to your database, the fruit picture appears in the Picture field.

- Demonstrate to students how to save the information entered into the *Fruit Pie* database by clicking the **Save** button on the **Forms** toolbar.

- Explain and demonstrate to your students how to use the database navigation buttons in the lower left-hand corner of the screen.

Special Note: Maximize the Fruit Data Entry Form, if necessary, to view the navigation buttons.

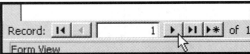

Also note that if each student will be working in his or her own database, then there won't be many records to navigate. However, it is still important for them to learn how to use the navigation buttons.

- Explain and demonstrate to your students how to print a single record in a database:
  - Click **File** on the **Menu** bar.
  - Click **Print**.
  - At the **Print** dialog box, click **Pages From** under **Print Range**.
  - Type the number of the record from the database that you want to print in both the **From** and **To** boxes, such as *1* and *1*.
  - Click **OK**.

Special Note: Students **should not** use the **Print** button on the **Forms** toolbar. A Print dialog box **will not** appear after clicking this button. The students will not have the opportunity to designate the record(s) they want printed. **All** the records in the database print when clicking the Print button. This may not be an issue if each student is creating his or her own database, but if the students are all working in one database, a lot of unnecessary printing will occur if they click the Print button.

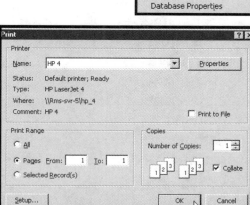

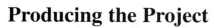

Producing the Project

Assign each student (or have each student select) a fruit to research. You will find a list of fruits to research above. The *Fruits to Research* resource file is also available on the CD-ROM [filename: **fruit3.doc**].

Fruits to Research

apple
apricot
avocado
banana
blueberry
cantaloupe
carambola
cherimoya
cherry
clementine
cranberry
date
durian
fig
grapefruit
grape
honeydew
kiwi
kumquat
lemon
lime
lychee
mandarin orange
mango
melon
nectarine
olive

orange
papaya
passion fruit
peach
pear
persimmon
pineapple
plum
pomegranate
raspberry
rock melon
strawberry
tangerine
watermelon

Once students complete their research, provide them with the opportunity to enter their findings into the *Fruit Pie* database. Be sure students understand how to find the database on the computer system, open the database, navigate the database, enter their information, save their work, and close the database.

Open the ***How to Make a "Fruit Pie"*** presentation file that is partially shown on the following page [filename: **fruit2.ppt**]. Show the presentation to students so they know how to make their own fruit pies. Then provide students with the opportunity to create their fruit pies.

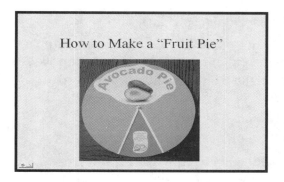

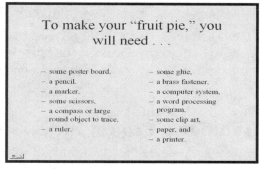

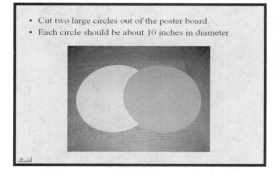

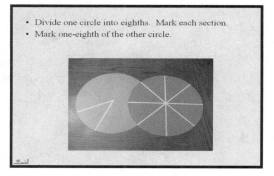

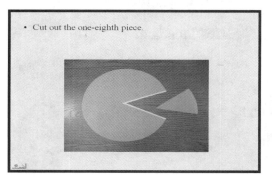

Hand out copies of the ***"Fruit Pie" Checklist and Score Sheet*** that is shown on the last page of this project [filename: **fruit4.doc**]. Explain to students how to use the checklist to keep them organized and aware of the grade they will receive upon completion of their fruit pies.

Presenting the Project

Congratulations! Your students collected fruit information and entered it into a *Microsoft Access* database. They used this information to create "fruit pies."

Each day, have a number of students present their fruit pies to the class. Presenters can explain the information displayed on each slice.

Display your students' fruit pies on the bulletin board in your classroom. Staple just the bottom part of each fruit pie onto the bulletin board, so that the top part can spin freely. That way, students can spin the fruit pies and view all of the information.

Additional Project Ideas

Now that students have a wealth of information about fruit at their fingertips, have them create a multimedia presentation about fruit. You can also create a fruit bulletin board or a mural to display what your students have learned.

Additional Resources

The following Internet sites and books will provide you with additional information and educational materials related to fruit:

Internet Sites

- Visit the USDA **The Food Guide Pyramid** to learn about the food groups, servings, and dietary guidelines. The Internet site address is:

  http://www.nal.usda.gov:8001/py/pmap.htm

- Visit **The Fruit Game** to play a fun fruit game. The Internet site address is:

  http://www.2020tech.com/fruit/

Internet Sites

- Visit the **Kid's Cookbook** site to learn how to make a fruit shake, as well as view other great recipes. The Internet site address is:

  http://www.dole5aday.com/CookBook/Break_Shake.html

- Visit **Cali's Kids** site to learn more about avocados. You will find teacher resources, including recipes, games, and coloring pages. The Internet site address is:

  http://www.avoinfo.com/kids/2000_54.php

Books

- *The Fruit Group* by Helen Frost was published in 2000 by Pebble Books [ISBN 0736805370].
- *A Fruit Is a Suitcase for Seeds* by Jean Richards was published in 2002 by Millbrook Press [ISBN 0761316221].
- *Cool As a Cucumber, Hot As a Pepper: Fruit Vegetables* by Meredith Sayles Hughes was published in 1998 by Lerner Publications Company [ISBN 0822528320].
- *Yes, We Have Bananas: Fruits from Shrubs and Vines* by Meredith Sayles Hughes was published in 1999 by Lerner Publications Company [ISBN 0822528363].
- *Tall and Tasty: Fruit Trees* by Meredith Sayles Hughes was published in 2000 by Lerner Publications Company [ISBN 08222526371].
- *Fruits* by Jackie Dwyer was published in 2001 by Powerkids Press [ISBN 0823956784].
- *At the Orchard* by Elizabeth Sirimarco was published in 1999 by Child's World [ISBN 1567665764].
- *A Kid's Guide to How Fruits Grow* by Patricia Ayers was published in 2000 by Powerkids Press [ISBN 0823954668].
- *Fruit and Vegetables* by Jenny Ridgwell was published in 1998 by Heineman Library [ISBN 1575726564].
- *Vegetables and Fruit* by Ro Drew was published in 1990 by Creative Teaching Press [ISBN 9991639039].

"Fruit Pie" Checklist and Score Sheet

Name   Date
_____

Fruit
_____

Directions: As you create your "fruit pie," check off your accomplishments. When you are finished, hand this checklist and "fruit pie" into your teacher for grading.

Check When Done	What to Do	Possible Points	My Score
	I cut two large circles out of poster board (approximately 10 inches in diameter)	10	
	I marked one-eighth of the first circle.	10	
	I cut out the one-eighth.	5	
	I divided the second circle into eighths.	10	
	I marked the eighths.	10	
	On the first circle (cover), I put the name of the fruit.	10	
	On the first circle, I put at least one picture of the fruit.	10	
	On the second circle, I placed an interesting fact in each slice.	40	
	Each fact included text and a picture.	40	
	My text is free of grammar, spelling, and punctuation errors.	40	
	I put the two circles together with the cover on top and punched a hole in the center.	5	
	I placed a brass fastener in the hole.	5	
	I put my name on the back of my "fruit pie."	5	
Total		200	

Musical Masters

So, who do you think was the greatest composer who ever lived? Was it Wolfgang Amadeus Mozart who wrote his first opera by the age of 12? Was it Ludwig Van Beethoven who composed profound musical works despite his loss of hearing? Or was it Richard Rodgers who in more recent times, teamed up with Oscar Hammerstein II to create Pulitzer Prize-winning musicals?

Project Description

Challenge your students to learn about the accomplishments of the great composers who have enriched our world with music with the following three-part project:

1. Students search the Web for information about well-known composers. They record the information, as well as links to the Internet sites they explored, in a *Microsoft Access* database.

2. Then each student creates a *Musical Masters* campaign poster that displays information about one composer. The information is designed to convince you to vote for him—or her—as the greatest composer who ever lived.

3. Finally, students share their posters and vote for their favorite composers. Certificates are presented to the first-, second-, and third-place winners of The Musical Masters Award.

Hardware and Software Needed

The following are the hardware and software applications you will need to complete the three project activities:

Gathering Musical Masters Data

For the first activity in this project, you will need your computer system and *Microsoft Access*. Since students will be completing their Musical Masters research on the Web, you will also need access to the Internet.

Creating Musical Masters Campaign Posters

For the second activity in this project, you will also need poster board—one piece for each student. If you want your students to create colorful components of their Musical Masters campaign poster on the computer (such as generating a picture of the composer, a banner, a border, and more), you will need your computer system and a word processing software application, such as *Microsoft Word*. You will also need a printer—preferably color. Then, you will also need a sufficient supply of scissors and glue so students can put it all together.

Presenting the Musical Masters Awards

For the third activity in this project, you can simply print *The Musical Masters Award for First Place* that is shown on this page. If you would like to provide second-, and third-place awards, you will need your computer system and *Microsoft PowerPoint*, so that you can open the file and print the additional certificates.

CD-ROM Files

The following files are provided to help you and your students complete this project. All of the files are available on the CD-ROM found in the back of this book.

Name of File	Description	Software Application	Filename on the CD-ROM
Musical Masters	database file	*Microsoft Access*	music.mdb
Musical Masters Sample	sample database file	*Microsoft Access*	musicsam.mdb
Musical Masters (to Research)	resource file	*Microsoft Word*	musicres.doc
Musical Masters Campaign Poster	sample poster file	*Microsoft Word*	poster.doc
Musical Masters Awards	awards resource file	*Microsoft PowerPoint*	award.ppt
Musical Masters Checklist and Score Sheet	organizer and score sheet	*Microsoft Word*	music2.doc

Materials Needed and File Preparation

The following are the materials you will need to obtain and the files you will need to prepare to complete the two project activities:

Gathering Musical Masters Data

Create a **Musical Masters Project** folder on the hard disk drive of each computer that will be used to complete this project. By creating this folder on each computer, you and your students will have a place to save all the files related to this project.

Special Note: If the computers that students will be using are connected via a network, locate the shared network drive and create a Musical Masters Project folder there. Once you place all the files needed for this project in this folder, students will be able to access the files from any computer connected to the network. Make sure however, that once students open a file, they save the file on the hard disk drive of their assigned computer or on a floppy disk.

- Send the ***Musical Masters*** database file [filename: **music.mdb**] that is found on the CD-ROM to the Musical Masters Project folder on every computer that will be used for this project. Be sure to also turn off the Read-only feature on the file on every computer. Alternatively, if the computers are networked, simply send the *Musical Masters* database file to the Musical Masters Project folder you set up on the shared drive, and turn off the Read-only feature on the file. (If you are not sure how to send the database file to a folder or how to turn off the Read-only feature, see the instructions in the Introduction section.)

Creating Musical Masters Campaign Posters

- Open the ***Musical Masters Campaign Poster*** sample file that is found on the CD-ROM [filename: **poster.doc**]. Save the file to the Musical Masters Project folder on each computer, or save each file to the network.

Presenting the Musical Masters Awards

- If you plan to present three awards—first, second, and third place—open the ***Musical Masters Awards*** file that is found on the CD-ROM [filename: **awards.ppt**]. Save the file to the Musical Masters Project folder on your computer.

Introducing the Project

Print or open and display the ***Musical Masters (to Research)*** file that is shown on the following page [filename: **musicres.doc**]. Assign or have each student select one of the musical masters to research.

Print or open and display the ***Musical Masters Campaign Poster*** that is shown on the following page [filename: **poster.doc**]. Discuss with students the purpose of the campaign poster. Have students identify the components of the campaign poster and determine how they contribute to the purpose.

Musical Masters

- Johann Sebastian Bach
- Béla Bartók
- Amy Beach
- Ludwig Van Beethoven
- Alban Berg
- Hector Berlioz
- Leonard Bernstein
- Georges Bizet
- Pierre Boulez
- Johannes Brahms
- John Cage
- Frédéric Chopin
- Aaron Copland
- George Crumb
- Claude Debussy
- Josquin Desprez
- Guillaume Du Fay
- Antonín Dvořák
- George Frideric Handel
- Lillian Hardin
- Franz Joseph Haydn
- Fanny Mendelssohn Hensel
- Elisabeth-Claude Jacquet de la Guerre
- Scott Joplin
- Paul Lansky
- Libby Larsen
- Ruggiero Leoncavallo
- György Ligeti
- Franz Liszt
- Witold Lutoslawski
- Guillaume de Machaut
- Gustav Mahler
- Felix Mendelssohn
- Olivier Messiaen
- Moniot d'Arras
- Claudio Monteverdi
- Wolfgang Amadeus Mozart
- Giovanni Pierluigi da Palestrina
- Sergei Prokofiev
- Henry Purcell
- Maurice Ravel
- Steve Reich
- Richard Rodgers
- Arnold Schoenberg
- Franz Peter Schubert
- Clara Wieck Schumann
- Robert Schumann
- Bedrich Smetana
- Richard Strauss
- Igor Stravinsky
- Antonio Vivaldi
- Giuseppe Verdi
- Hildegard von Bingen
- Richard Wagner
- Anton Webern

Inform students that they will be creating campaign posters similar to this one in their **Musical Masters** project. Explain to students that the Musical Masters project contains three activities:

- First, students will collect data about their composers and enter the information they find in a *Microsoft Access* database. The information they will gather about each composer includes his or her name, the year the composer was born, the year the composer died (if he or she is no longer living), the country where the composer was born, the major contributions the composer made to the world of music, and the links to Internet sites where the information was found.
- Second, students will use the information they gathered to create campaign posters that display information about the composers.
- Third, based upon the information presented in the campaign posters, the students will vote to determine who is the greatest composer.

First show the students an example of a completed *Musical Masters* database:

- Launch *Microsoft Access*.
- Open the *Musical Masters Sample* database file from the CD-ROM [filename: **musicsam.mdb**].

    Special Note: A dialog box will appear informing you that the database is Read-only. This is fine since you will only be viewing, not changing, this sample database. Click **OK**.

- At the **musicsam** database dialog box, click **Forms** under the **Objects Bar**.
- Click **Composers** under the **Objects** list.
- Click **Open**.

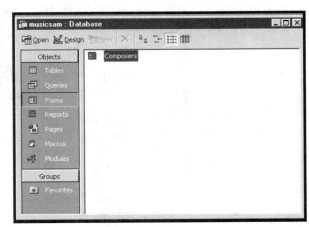

- The **Composers** table, displayed in **Form View**, will appear on your screen.

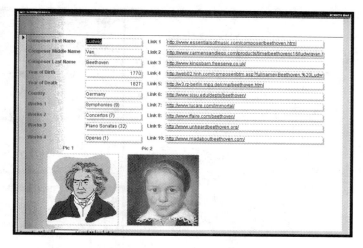

- Explain to students that this is a sample Composers form. They will be creating one just like it with information that they gather about a particular composer.

- Explain and demonstrate the features of Composers form as follows:
  - Explain to students that the words in blue text are the names of fields in the database. Elicit from students the names of the fields they see, such as Composer First Name, Composer Middle Name, and more.
  - Explain to students that the white text boxes with the yellow borders next to the labels are where they will enter information about each composer.

- Take a moment to view some of the example data on the composer Ludwig Van Beethoven. Point out the Internet addresses and pictures as well.

- Close the ***Musical Masters Sample*** database file.

- Now open and demonstrate to students how to use the *Musical Masters* database file template. Here's how:

- Open the ***Musical Masters*** database file from your Musical Masters Project folder [filename: **music.mdb**].

  Special Note: Prior to opening the file, be sure that the Read-only feature is turned off.

- At the **music** database dialog box, click **Forms** under the **Objects Bar**.
- Click the **Composers** form under the **Objects** list.
- Click **Open**.

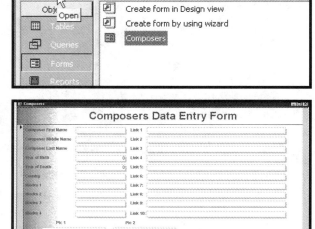

An empty **Composers** table, displayed in **Form View**, will appear on your screen.

Using the data provided in the instructions below, explain and demonstrate how students should enter data into each field as follows:

- Click in the **Composer First Name** field and type the first name of your composer, such as *Ludwig*. Then press the **<Enter>** key or **<Tab>** key on your keyboard to move to the next field.
- In the **Composer Middle Name** field, type the middle name of your composer, such as *Van*. Then press the **<Enter>** key or **<Tab>** key on your keyboard to move to the next field.
- In the **Composer Last Name** field, type the last name of your composer, such as *Beethoven*. Then press the **<Enter>** key or **<Tab>** key on your keyboard to move to the next field.
- In the **Year of Birth** field, type the year your composer was born, such as *1770*. Then press the **<Enter>** key or **<Tab>** key on your keyboard to move to the next field.
- In the **Year of Death** field, type the year your composer died, such as *1827*. Then press the **<Enter>** key or **<Tab>** key on your keyboard to move to the next field.
- In the **Country** field, type the name of the country where your composer was born, such as *Germany*. Then press the **<Enter>** key or **<Tab>** key on your keyboard to move to the next field.

- In the **Works 1** through **Works 4** fields, type information about the musical works that your composer created, such as ***Symphonies (9)***. Then press the **<Enter>** key or **<Tab>** key on your keyboard to move to the next field.
- In the **Link 1** through **Link 10** fields, copy and paste the URLs (Internet addresses) of the Web pages where you obtained information about your composer, such as
http://www.essentialsofmusic.com/composer/beethoven.html
Then press the **<Enter>** key or **<Tab>** key on your keyboard to move to the next field.
- In the **Pic 1** and **Pic 2** fields, enter pictures that you find of your composer from the *Microsoft Clip Gallery* or the Internet, such as those you saw in the *Musical Masters Sample* database.

Special Note: There are several ways you can insert pictures into the **Pic 1** and **Pic 2** fields. Here are two ways—clip art and saved picture files:

To insert clip art from the *Microsoft* Clip Gallery:

- Click on the **Pic 1** picture box to select it.
- Click **Insert** on the **Menu** bar.
- Click **Object**.

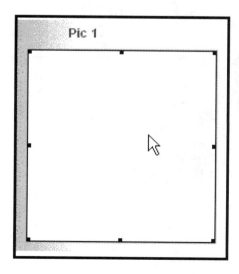
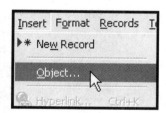

- At the **Insert Object** dialog box, click **Create New**.

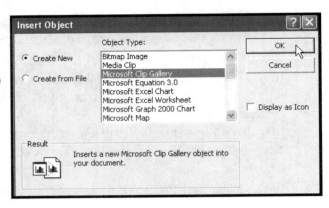

- Click **Microsoft Clip Gallery** under **Object Type**.

- Click **OK**.

- At the **Microsoft Clip Gallery** dialog box, navigate to a picture of your composer.

Special Note: If you don't find a picture of your composer in the *Microsoft Clip Gallery*, you can click the **Clips Online** button. If your Web browser is active, you will be taken to the *Microsoft Office Design Gallery Live*. You can search for a picture of your composer there. When you find it, you can select it and download it into your *Microsoft Clip Gallery*.

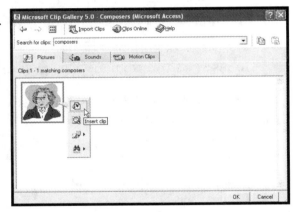

- Click the picture of your composer to select it.

- Click the **Insert clip** button.

- When you return to the your database form, you will see your composer in the **Pic 1** field.

To insert a saved picture:

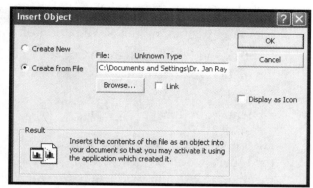

- Click on the **Pic 2** picture box to select it.

- Click **Insert** on the **Menu** bar.

- Click **Object**.

- At the **Insert Object** dialog box, click **Create from File**.

- Then click the **Browse** button to navigate to your picture file.

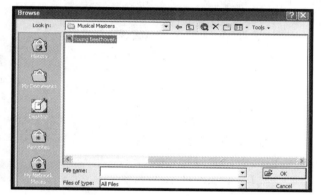

- At the **Browse** dialog box, click the **Look in** list arrow and navigate to the folder where you saved your composer picture file.

- Click the picture file to select it.

- Click **OK**.

- When you return to the **Insert Object** dialog box, simply click **OK** again.

- When you return to the your database form, you will see your composer in the **Pic 2** field.

- Demonstrate to students how to save the information entered into the database by clicking the **Save** button on the **Forms** toolbar.
- Explain and demonstrate to your students how to use the database navigation buttons in the lower left-hand corner of the screen.

  Special Note: Maximize the Composers form if necessary to view the navigation buttons.

  Also note that if each student will be working in his or her own database, then there won't be many records to navigate. However, it is still important for them to learn how to use the navigation buttons.

  - Explain and demonstrate to your students how to print a single record in a database. Here's how:
  - Click **File** on the **Menu** bar.
  - Click **Print**.
  - At the **Print** dialog box, click **Pages From** under **Print Range**.
  - Type the number of the record from the database that you want to print in both the **From** and **To** boxes, such as *1* and *1*.
  - Click **OK**.

Special Note: Students **should not** use the **Print** button on the **Forms** toolbar. A Print dialog box **will not** appear after clicking this button. The students will not have the opportunity to designate the record(s) they want printed. **All** the records in the database print when clicking the Print button. This may not be an issue if each student is creating his or her own database, but if the students are all working in one database, a lot of unnecessary printing will occur if they click the Print button.

Producing the Project

Assign each student (or have each student select) a composer to research. You will find a list of the musical masters on page 180. The *Musical Masters (to Research)* resource file is also available on the CD-ROM [filename: **musicres.doc**].

Once students complete their research, provide them with the opportunity to enter their findings into the *Musical Masters* database. Be sure students understand how to find the database on the computer system, open the database, navigate the database, enter their information, save their work, and close the database.

Once students enter their Musical Masters information into the database, provide them with the opportunity to create their Musical Masters campaign posters. Pass out copies of the *Musical Masters Checklist and Score Sheet* that is shown on the last page of this project [filename: **music2.doc**]. Explain to students how to use this handout to guide their Musical Masters campaign poster creations. For practice, you can even have students use the *Musical Masters Checklist and Score Sheet* to evaluate the sample poster.

Presenting the Project

Congratulations! Your students collected composer information and entered it in a *Microsoft Access* database. They used this information as a foundation for creating Musical Masters campaign posters. Now it is time for students to cast their votes.

Each day, have a number of students present their Musical Masters campaign posters to the class. Presenters can explain the information displayed on their posters, as well as share additional interesting facts that they learned during their research.

Then display all the Musical Masters campaign posters and allow students the opportunity to vote for the composer they consider the greatest who ever lived. You may need to have a run-off election after the field is narrowed to five or six composers.

After the final elections, provide the top winner with The Musical Masters Award certificate that is shown below. You can also provide The Musical Masters Award certificates to the second- and third-place winners. All three certificates are available in the ***Musical Masters Awards*** file on the CD-ROM [filename: **award.ppt**]. Simply open this file and type in the winning composer's name on each certificate. Then print and sign The Musical Masters Award certificates and affix them to the winning posters.

Additional Project Ideas

Now that students have learned about the great composers, see how many of their musical pieces you and your students can collect. Try to find and listen to at least one piece from each composer researched. Keep these pieces in the listening center in your classroom for students to enjoy.

Post your *Musical Masters* database file on your classroom Web site. Then your students' family members and friends, as well as other students from around the world, can view the Musical Masters information.

Design and create your own *Microsoft Access* database of musical instruments. Just as with the composers, have each student select an instrument about which to learn.

Gather the information, as well as pictures of the instruments, into a *Musical Instruments* database. Based upon the information gathered, have students create musical instrument mobiles.

Additional Resources

The following Internet sites and books will provide you with additional information and educational materials related to the great composers:

Internet Sites

- Visit this ThinkQuest **Composers** site to view information about the composers Johann Bach, Wolfgang Mozart, George Gershwin, and more. The Internet site address is:

  http://www.thinkquest.org/library/lib/site_sum_outside.html?tname=4004&cid=2&url=4004/

- Visit the **Classical Composer Archives** to see which great composer was born on today's date, as well as search the archives for information about your chosen composer. The Internet site address is:

  http://voyager.physics.unlv.edu/webpages2/picgalr2.html

- Visit this ThinkQuest **Cool Composers** site to view information about the composers Bach, Beethoven, Bizet, Haydn, Mozart, and Tchaikovsky. The Internet site address is:

  http://www.thinkquest.org/library/lib/site_sum_outside.html?tname=5399&cid=2&url=5399/

- Visit the **Essentials of Music** site. You will find information about 70 composers. Plus, you can listen to audio excerpts of their music. The Internet site address is:

  http://essentialsofmusic.com/

- Visit the New York Philharmonic **KidZone**. Click the link to the Composer's Gallery where you will find quizzes and puzzles and more. The Internet site address is:

  http://www.nyphilkids.org/main.phtml

- Visit the ThinkQuest **The Symphony—An Interactive Guide** site. You will find a timeline of composers and compositions, a complete guide to instruments in an orchestra, and information about composers. The Internet site address is:

http://www.thinkquest.org/library/lib/site_sum_outside.html?tname=22673&url=22673/

- Visit the PBS **Continental Harmony** site. You will find a sound lounge, a teacher's guide, and more. At this site, you can even create your own musical arrangements. The Internet site address is:

http://www.pbs.org/harmony/

Books

- *Composers* by David Bouchier was published in 1999 by Black Dog and Leventhal Publishers [ISBN 0761112065].

- *Story of the Orchestra—Listen While You Learn About the Instruments, Music, and the Composers Who Wrote the Music!* By Meredith Hamilton was published in 2000 by Black Dog and Leventhal Publishers [ISBN 1579121489].

- *Great Composers* by Stuart Kallen was published in 2000 by Lucent Books [ISBN 1560066695].

- *Ten Great American Composers* by Carmen Bredeson was published in 2002 by Enslow Publishers [ISBN 0766018326].

- *American Composers* by Eric Tomb was published in 1992 by Bellerophon Books [ISBN 0883881586].

- *Bach to Rock—Introduction to Famous Composers and Their Music with Related Activities* by Rosemary Kennedy was published in 1983 by Rosemary Corporation [ISBN 0962195200].

Glossary

Access—See *Microsoft Access*.

Access **Window**—See *Microsoft Access* Window.

Asterisk—a *Microsoft Access* symbol that appears next to a blank record at the end of the database table. The asterisk indicates that this is the next record you will use to enter information.

CD-ROM—Compact Disc-Read Only memory is the circular disk that stores files in digital form. It can be accessed to open files just like a floppy disk drive and hard drive.

Click—the action you perform when you push a button on the mouse to position your cursor, select an item, or activate a *Microsoft Access* feature.

Close Button—the small square button with the X in it at the top right-hand side of your screen. Clicking on this button closes the *Microsoft Access* program.

Close Window Button—the small square button with the X in it at the right end of the Menu bar. It is identical to and located just below the Close button. Clicking this button closes the database you are no longer using.

Common Field—a field that appears in two or more tables. A common field allows you to connect records between or among tables.

Copy—the process of selecting numbers and/or text and placing them in memory for pasting in another location. When you copy, the original numbers and/or text you selected remains the same.

Current Record—is the record within the database table on which you are currently working.

Cursor—the symbol displayed on the computer screen (a blinking bar, an I-beam, an arrowhead, or other icon) that indicates where your next keystroke will appear in your worksheet.

Cut—to remove text or numbers from your document.

Database—an organized collection of information. In *Microsoft Access* the database is organized into related tables.

Database Management System (DBMS)—a software application, such as *Microsoft Access*, that enables you to store, retrieve, sort, and analyze data within a database. It also allows you to print the information.

Database Window—the window that appears when you open a *Microsoft Access* database file. It is the main control center for working with the open database file.

Datasheet View—one of two ways to view a *Microsoft Access* table. The Datasheet View is used to enter information into the database table.

DBMS—see Database Management System.

Default—how the settings are automatically set up in *Microsoft Access*. For example, the default Data Type is Text.

Delete—to remove text or numbers from a database.

Delete Key—a key on your keyboard that erases items on your screen. When you press the delete key, the text or numbers to the right of the cursor are cleared. If text or numbers in your database are selected, when you press the delete key, the entire highlighted area is cleared.

Design View—one of two ways to view a *Microsoft Access* table. Design View is used to design and modify the database table.

Dialog Box—a box that appears on your screen that prompts you to provide some type of input, such as text or values, or that prompts you to make a selection or click a button.

Exit—a drop-down menu item that allows you to quit the *Microsoft Access* program when selected.

Field—an attribute of a person, place, object, event, or idea. Some of the fields in a student database may be student ID number, student first name, student last name, and student birth date. The columns within a database table are called fields.

Field Name—the name of a field within a table. The column headings within a database table are called field names.

Field Value—the specific value or content of a field.

File—a document that is stored on your computer, floppy diskette, or CD-ROM. In *Microsoft Access*, a file is also known as a database.

Filename—the name you give a file upon saving it.

Font—the typeface of letters formed as you enter text in your database, such as Times New Roman or Arial.

Foreign Key—the primary key in a database table that becomes a field in a second table.

Form—a *Microsoft Access* database object used to develop an attractive way to enter, display, and print the information in a table.

Formatting—working with the attributes of text and design features in the database on your screen, such as resizing, bolding, and entering text.

Groups Bar—the section of the Database Window that allows you to group database objects so they are easier to work with. It also allows you to create shortcuts to those objects.

Hardware—the parts of your computer that you can see and touch.

Highlight—when the mouse is dragged over text or numbers in a database, they become highlighted. The highlighting indicates that they are selected and ready to be manipulated.

Icon—a small image on your computer screen used to represent a specific program or to initiate an action in *Microsoft Access*.

Internet—an International web of computer networks.

Key Field—a field that is common to two or more tables within a database.

Launch—to open a software program, such as *Microsoft Access*, so you can use it.

Macro—a *Microsoft Access* database object used to develop commands that automate the performance of repetitive tasks.

Menu—a list of available options.

Menu bar—the set of menu items, such as File, Edit, and View, displayed at the top of the *Microsoft Access* screen.

Microsoft Access—a database software application that allows you to enter, maintain, and retrieve information.

Microsoft Access **Window**—the program window that appears when you start the *Microsoft Access* program.

Microsoft Windows—operating system software that helps the PC (personal computer) carry out tasks, such as displaying information on the computer screen and saving your files.

Module—a *Microsoft Access* database object used to automate repetitive database tasks through programming in Visual Basic for Applications.

Objects Bar—the section of the Database Window that displays the major object groups—Tables, Queries, Forms, Reports, Pages, Macros, and Modules.

Page—a *Microsoft Access* database object used to develop an HTML document that can be posted on your classroom Web site.

Pencil—a *Microsoft Access* symbol that indicates two things—what record you are working on and that the record has not been saved.

Primary Key—a field whose value uniquely identifies each record in a table. In a student database, the student ID number would serve as the primary key, as it uniquely identifies each student record.

Query—a *Microsoft Access* database object used to provide answers to questions about information within the database. First a query specifies a set of criteria and then it searches the database for information that satisfies the criteria.

Relational Database—a collection of related tables.

Relational Database Management System—a database management system with data organized into a collection of tables with relationships formed among common fields.

Record—a set of field values. In a student database, the information for each student is stored as a separate record. The rows within a database table are called records.

Record Selector Symbol—a symbol, such as a triangle, an asterisk, or a pencil that indicates the status of a record.

Report—a *Microsoft Access* database object used to provide the data in an attractive fashion in printed form.

Save—the pull-down menu item or button on the Standard toolbar that allows you to store your workbook on the hard drive or on your floppy diskette.

Table—a collection of data about a person, place, object, event, or idea. It is made up of records and fields. A database table looks very similar to a spreadsheet. The rows in the table are records and the columns in the table are fields.

Template—a way to save a database file so that you can use its structure over and over again.

Triangle—a *Microsoft Access* symbol that indicates that the record has been saved.

CD-ROM Index

Page Number in Text	Name of Section or Project	Title of the File	Description	Software Application	Filename on the CD-ROM
9	**Introduction**	*Additional Resources*	Resource file	*Microsoft Word*	addresc.doc
18	**Getting Started**	Classroom Software Library	database file	*Microsoft Access*	software.mdb
87	**Creating Your Own** *Microsoft Access* **Database**	*Saluting the States Sample*	sample database	*Microsoft Access*	statessam.mdb
105	**The Wonder of Whales**	*Whales Internet Sites*	resource file	*Microsoft Word*	whaleint.doc
106	**The Wonder of Whales**	*Whales*	database file	*Microsoft Access*	whales.mdb
106	**The Wonder of Whales**	*A Whale of a Cinquain Poem*	student writing prompt template	*Microsoft Word*	cinquain.dot
106	**The Wonder of Whales**	*A Handsome Whale Haiku*	student writing prompt template	*Microsoft Word*	haiku.dot
106	**The Wonder of Whales**	*A Cute Whale Quatrain*	student writing prompt template	*Microsoft Word*	quatrain.dot
106	**The Wonder of Whales**	*A Laughable Whale Limerick*	student writing prompt template	*Microsoft Word*	limerick.dot

CD-ROM Index *(cont.)*

Page Number in Text	Name of Section or Project	Title of the File	Description	Software Application	Filename on the CD-ROM
106	**The Wonder of Whales**	*The Wonder of Whales—A Collection of Poetry Sample*	presentation file	*Microsoft PowerPoint*	whalessam.ppt
106	**The Wonder of Whales**	*The Wonder of Whales—A Collection of Poetry Template*	presentation file	*Microsoft PowerPoint*	whalestem.ppt
107	**The Wonder of Whales**	*Whales Sample*	sample database file	*Microsoft Access*	whalesam.mdb
115	**The Wonder of Whales**	*Whales to Research*	resource file	*Microsoft Word*	whalesre.doc
126	**Saluting the States**	*Saluting the States*	database file	*Microsoft Access*	states.mdb
126	**Saluting the States**	*Saluting the States Sample*	database file sample	*Microsoft Access*	statessam.mdb
127	**Saluting the States**	State Populations	sample chart	*Microsoft Excel*	statepop.xls
127	**Saluting the States**	*State Sizes*	sample chart	*Microsoft Excel*	statesiz.xls
127	**Saluting the States**	*People*	clip art file		people.bmp
127	**Saluting the States**	*Scene*	clip art file		scene.bmp
129	**Saluting the States**	*Saluting the States Research Organizer*	student research organizer	*Microsoft Word*	statesorg.doc

CD-ROM Index *(cont.)*

Page Number in Text	Name of Section or Project	Title of the File	Description	Software Application	Filename on the CD-ROM
134	**Saluting the States**	*Fifty States to Research*	resource file	*Microsoft Word*	50states.doc
151	**Presidential Portraits**	*The Presidents*	database file	*Microsoft Access*	pres1.mdb
151	**Presidential Portraits**	*How to Make a Presidential Portrait*	presentation file	*Microsoft PowerPoint*	pres2.ppt
151	**Presidential Portraits**	*Presidential Portrait Checklist and Score Sheet*	organizer and score sheet file	*Microsoft Word*	pres4.doc
152	**Presidential Portraits**	*The Presidents Sample*	sample database file	*Microsoft Access*	pressam.mdb
164	**Presidential Portraits**	*Presidents to Research*	resource file	*Microsoft Word*	pres3.doc
172	**Guess the Great Invention**	*Inventions*	database file	*Microsoft Access*	invent.mdb
173	**Guess the Great Invention**	*Guess Which Invention I Am Sample*	sample presentation file	*Microsoft PowerPoint*	invensam.ppt
173	**Guess the Great Invention**	*Guess Which Invention I Am Template*	presentation template file	*Microsoft PowerPoint*	inventem.ppt
174	**Guess the Great Invention**	*Inventions Sample*	sample database file	*Microsoft Access*	inventsa.mdb
184	**Guess the Great Invention**	*Inventions to Research*	resource file	*Microsoft Word*	invenres.doc

CD-ROM Index *(cont.)*

Page Number in Text	Name of Section or Project	Title of the File	Description	Software Application	Filename on the CD-ROM
195	**Fruit Pie**	*Fruit Pie*	database file	*Microsoft Access*	fruit1.mdb
195	**Fruit Pie**	*How to Make a "Fruit Pie"*	presentation file	*Microsoft PowerPoint*	fruit2.ppt
195	**Fruit Pie**	*"Fruit Pie" Checklist and Score Sheet*	organizer and score sheet	*Microsoft Word*	fruit4.doc
198	**Fruit Pie**	*Fruit Pie Sample*	sample database file	*Microsoft Access*	fruitsa.mdb
207	**Fruit Pie**	*Fruits to Research*	resource file	*Microsoft Word*	fruit3.doc
216	**Musical Masters**	*Musical Masters*	database file	*Microsoft Access*	music.mdb
216	**Musical Masters**	*Musical Masters Campaign Poster*	sample poster file	*Microsoft Word*	poster.doc
216	**Musical Masters**	*Musical Masters Awards*	awards resource file	*Microsoft PowerPoint*	award.ppt
216	**Musical Masters**	Musical Masters (to Research)	resource file	*Microsoft Word*	musicres.doc
218	**Musical Masters**	Musical Masters Sample	sample database file	*Microsoft Access*	musicsam.mdb
225	**Musical Masters**	*Musical Masters Checklist and Score Sheet*	organizer and score sheet	*Microsoft Word*	music2.doc

Notes:

238